THE
RESTLESS HEART

THE
RESTLESS HEART

Breaking the Cycle of Social Identity

by

Robert C. Harvey

WILLIAM B. EERDMANS PUBLISHING COMPANY
GRAND RAPIDS, MICHIGAN

Library of Congress Cataloging in Publication Data

Harvey, Robert C
  The restless heart: breaking the cycle of social
identity.

  Includes bibliographical references.
  1. Individualism. 2. Identity (Psychology).
  3. Social ethics. 4. Sociology, Christian.
I. Title.
HM131.H33   301.11   72-94607
ISBN 0-8028-1507-3

To
Royden Keith Yerkes

"Thou hast formed us for thyself, and our heart is restless till it rests in thee."

Augustine *Confessions* i.1.

PREFACE

The sense of individual identity that has been the foundation stone of Western culture for nearly eight hundred years has, within the space of two or three generations, nearly expired. This is what lies behind the identity crisis of our day. It is the real death that has brought about the suppositious death of God.

In other times than ours the individual was shaped by his developing participation in various groups—especially the family, the school, and the Church. Once he learned to function responsibly within these groups, his identity began to acquire a clear delineation. It was enlarged and clarified as he took part in additional, specialized groups. In other days, those groups gave his life depth and meaning. Today they do not. Neither in the groups to which he belongs nor in himself does the modern individual appear in sharp focus. As a result he can no longer act with fluency and power.

This book is intended to provide an understanding of human identity, and of the crisis it is going through. It is particularly concerned with freedom and responsibility, and with the way they touch the individual in his relation to the group. At the outset two terms may be clarified—*personality* and *identity*. The Latin *persona, a mask,* seems to connote the character one displays in public, rather than the inner self. In this sense, personality is the study of psychiatry, which seeks to reconcile the outer mask with the inner self. Our concern will be with the person behind the mask, and with outlining a conscious self-identification. *Identity* will be used in its sense of distinguishing one individual and one group from all others. It is a subtle word, for its Latin root, *idem, the same*, suggests that identity may be shared as well as retained—diffused as well as delineated. An identical twin's difficulty is that people confuse him with his brother. Visitors at the bedside of a sick friend tend to overidentify with him in his suffering, thereby losing the power to be separate and helpful selves. To be real, personality must always possess id entity.

We shall treat the subject by studying the various social and religious forms that shape and express social personality. There are only a few. Although these forms may seem casual and even accidental, they are deeply rooted in the human psyche. As such, I believe they have universal application.

Personhood is discovered in the biblical idea that God is a person, and that man, being created in His image, is also personal. It comes with the Judeo-Christian experience of the divine-human confrontation. Other religions are not only impersonal; some have the effect of depersonalizing man. It seems to me that the patterns described here are the only ones by which men and societies can mold social personality. Using them as a guide, one might achieve a fairly well-balanced set of personality traits. However, the person that took shape would not be real, but a *persona*. It is not in mimicking patterns that we become real, but in relating to persons and ideas. The social and religious groups to which we are member largely determine what we shall be in relation to others. What we shall be within our selves is entirely up to us.

The material in this book is not particularly difficult; but if along the way confusion should arise regarding the different social identity types, the reader is encouraged to refer to the summary charts on pp. 89ff.

CONTENTS

Chapter One

THE DILEMMA
OF WESTERN MAN

W. H. Auden has called our era "The Age of Anxiety."
It is an apt description. We live in a time that is both
thrilling and chilling. Our leapfrog advances in science have
opened myriad possibilities for civilization, yet the ensuing
difficulties threaten not only our social gains, but life
itself. One problem is virtually unnoticed because it is the
most elemental of all: what we are and what we are
becoming. In the five decades since World War I the
popular assumptions about social character have undergone a radical readjustment, and the change has hardly
been detected. We have become unwitting participants in a
silent process of un-becoming.

Even in the way we feel about it, it is a complex time.
Among the new nations there is an emergence of real
individuality, to the accompaniment of joy and creative
expression. This is something that has not been experienced here in the West for many centuries. We are beset by
an anxiety that betokens a massive erosion of identity. The
causes of this erosion are subtle, but they can still be seen
by those who have some understanding of what social
character is all about.

Dimensions of the Crisis

Actually, there are two identity crises, the individual's
and the group's. The group's crisis stems from the lack of

wholeness in its members, the individual's from lack of integrity in the group. The experience is the more terrifying for the individual, because it is in him that life, in its essence, is found. Even so, the character and the quality of the individual's life can be derived only from membership in the group.

Today's individual is incomplete because he has never belonged to a real, life-giving group. He has no real values and convictions of his own. No one has given him the myths and symbols and traditions that every society needs. He has never learned to discriminate between what is life-sustaining and what is life-destroying. He lacks a sense of achievement and of self-respect. He has no clear and definable sense of self, and of larger mission and purpose. Both as an individual and as a member of society he is moribund in the things that pertain to personhood. This is his predicament, and it is that of Western man.

Let us consider how, in the past, individuality has taken shape. It has arisen through man's private responses to the possibilities of freedom. This has required the experience of living—and, moreover, of living accountably. The individual discovered himself in the choices he had to make, and in the mistakes he had to make up for. His identity was his private history of responsible encounter.

Before this could take place, however, the individual had to earn his freedom. He had to pass the tests of behavior, meeting the standards of the group. He had to accept, in a time of training and trial, the standards and controls by which the group regulates personhood in its members. The individual had to merit the right to personhood, but it was the group that decided what personhood was.

Failure of Individual and *Group*

Social personality has always preceded individual identity. Until the group is free and accountable in itself it cannot point the way to personhood for its members. This, at least, has been the case until now. In our time the group has lost the sense of identity that makes it definable to itself and to others. Its concern for itself has led it to withhold the most important aspects of its *members'* personhood. It no longer allows them to be responsible for their decisions—or even to make decisions. This means that the group no longer considers the individual to be a person. More and more it thinks of itself as being the basic person in society. It regards grouphood as the lowest common denominator in personhood. Yet it is evident that in the West real personhood is seldom found either in the individual or in the group. We are becoming a culture of un-persons.

The chief cause of this is a decline in the power of religion. Christianity is no longer able to give the cosmic orientation men once had. In the time when Christendom was—for most men—the world, men were baptized into the Church's concepts even when they rejected its faith. They could not help themselves. The concepts were the culture. Men absorbed them as by osmosis, without even knowing it. Today this is no longer true. We are a pluralistic society, whose basic concepts are not Christian, but pagan. Christianity has had to take its place as one of many available options. Not only does it have a lessened influence on those who call themselves Christians. It is no longer expected by outsiders to give stability to the entire social order. The upshot is that there is no longer an orientation that all men must adopt. Increasingly, there is no orientation that any men *may* adopt. The cosmic rules have seemingly disappeared. Men must now make up their own.

The rules of personhood—the man-made as well as the intrinsic—are the subject of this study. Some of our chapters will deal with the evolution of identity's various forms. Others will consider a social psychology by which renewal may be sought. The present chapter, while touching the symptoms and causes of our culture's crisis, can hardly touch them all. Some of our material must be dealt with later as the history itself unfolds.

The disintegration of personhood is illustrated in the changing American scene. At one point we were a society of individuals. Now we are not. Our early immigrants had an individualism that was rooted in their religion. They brought with them their Protestant ethic of industry, frugality, and thrift. What hardships they endured only heightened the resourcefulness they had acquired across the sea. Their identities were enhanced by their having started out with almost nothing. Yet it was enough. They had their God, they had themselves, and they had a love of work and order. They transformed the wilderness and built a great society. Even though that society's concept of itself was individualistic, it had a strong social personality. Its members came from well-defined mold. By contrast, today's society is unable to produce what it values most—a viable group. It denies the attributes of personhood to its members, but it has failed to come up with a social personality of its own.

A Case History from the Korean War

One of the first clear signs of failure in American life came in a psychological study of returning prisoners at the end of the Korean War. The study revealed some shocking facts. More than two-thirds of the men captured had submitted to brainwashing and indoctrination. More than a third were guilty of serious collaboration with the enemy or of criminal treatment of fellow prisoners. Ninety percent were so disoriented that they had to undergo psychiatric treatment upon their return home. Only ten percent had been able, while in captivity, to keep their personal integrity.

Other figures were equally alarming. Thirty-eight percent of the Americans taken had died in captivity—the largest percentage of any war. Two dozen chose not to return; they were the only sizeable number of turncoats the United States had ever known. Finally, for the first time, not one prisoner was able to escape and rejoin his forces. Those who tried to do so either were captured, or were betrayed by their fellows, or they lost heart and turned themselves in.

The study made it evident that from the beginning the once resourceful American had lost his bearings and drive. From the moment of capture, morale disappeared. Officers lost their authority. The rank and file surrendered their common sense. The marches to prison camp became death marches because the wounded would not help themselves and no one would come to their aid. A sense of helplessness prevailed throughout the months of captivity. As one middle-aged prisoner—a medical officer—remarked, the general attitude was not the old, "What can I do to help myself?" but rather, "What can be done to help me?"[1]

The disorientation was more than one of discipline and morale. It was also one of survival. When there was food and clothing, the strong took it. When fuel was limited, the sick were rolled out into the cold to die. Men froze because too few were willing to forage for firewood. The largest number of deaths, however, came from malnutrition—and quite unnecessarily. Men turned up their noses at a soybean diet, in which the needed nutrients were provided. They chose to live on rice alone, and so were more vulnerable to disease and finally death.

A far different experience was undergone by a regiment of Turks, who were also captured by the Chinese. From the outset it was made clear to their captors that all orders had to be given to the ranking Turkish officer. No prisoner would obey an order that did not come from his own superior. As a result, the Turks maintained good discipline and morale throughout their captivity. While on the march, two able men were assigned to carry each wounded soldier. In the Death Valley Camp, where the 229 Turks and some 1600 Americans were detained while the Chinese were building other prisons, all the Turks survived. By contrast, six hundred Americans died there.

The Turks' superior discipline continued until the war's end. They shared alike in food and clothing, and in whatever else could be provided. Every able man worked as best he could. The sick were assigned nurses from among their own comrades, and all returned to health. Not one Turk was brainwashed. Not one was guilty of collaboration. Not one died in captivity. None had to be given psychiatric reorientation upon their return home. Every man had kept his integrity.

How is one to explain the difference? Superficial answers are not enough. At heart was a radical difference in their sense of identity. The Americans were members of a society in which *individual* personhood is crumbling, and in which the substitute—*collective* personality— is inadequate to meet the needs of existence. The Turks were members of a *corporate* culture that offers constancy in membership, secure values and discipline, and a sense of mutual involvement and concern. As captives in a strange and intimidating environment, the Turks knew how to behave. The Americans, on the other hand, were easily disoriented from reality. Their identities were already weak, and the communists' treatment brought further disintegration. They gave up and died—psychically as well as physically.

As a result of the Korean experience, the armed forces made important changes in the training of recruits. They no longer assumed the inventiveness and self-sufficiency of the American male. They began to train their personnel, not only in the rules of conventional warfare, but in every art of survival. As a result there was not, in Vietnam, a repetition of Korea.

Yet the problem at home is growing. Increasingly, young Americans are stunted in the freedom, responsibility, and obedience that only a secure environment can give. Every institution that is supposed to serve them is itself in a state of crisis—the family, the university, the State, the Church. None has ever been more impotent in meeting the needs of the young. Yet the current crisis is in part due to a failure of the young people as well. The existence of a counterculture is due not so much to the wickedness of the Establishment as to a shift in man's sense of identity. Men no longer make a universal assumption of individual responsibility. Rather, they reject the very idea of personal accountability.

Protection for the Individual

It is significant that the individual's psychic failure has quickened a great deal of concern for his rights. Much of our recent legislation has been designed to protect the individual. It has protected him from invasion of his privacy. It has protected him from the consequences of his actions. These laws have laid down a smokescreen to hide the fact that, as a person, the individual is nearly defunct. This becomes clear when we realize that during the centuries of individualism there were no laws at all to protect the individual's privacy. There were but few to protect his rights. If we reflect on this, we can see the reason. Egrets need protection. Starlings can take care of themselves.

An accompaniment to the demise of individual identity is the virtual end, in the Western world, of capital punishment. Yet this does not mean that Western sympathies have enlarged. It means that we have swallowed the doctrine of behaviorism. We have accepted the idea that a killer is not wicked, but merely sick. Believing this, we cannot treat him as responsible. We cannot, therefore, give him the punishment that a different sense of justice seems to require.

While the death penalty's abolition may indeed say something about our compassion, it offers one enormous insult to the human race. It says that there is nothing a man can do that is worth his life. It implies that no man is wholly a person, and therefore subject to the justice that his own conscience may require. It says that society can require no ultimate obligation of its members. We still claim the right to take a man's liberty, but—at this point— no longer his life.

Exchange of Ethical Absolutes

We come to a phenomenon that few, if any, have ever drawn attention to. It is an unprecedented change in morality that has taken place in the space of a single generation. In the years since World War II there has been an exchange of moral absolutes from the field of individual ethics to that of public ethics. Conversely, there has been an exchange of moral relativities from the field of public ethics to that of private ethics.

Throughout the ages of individualism it was held that the individual was governed by a set of divinely given absolutes. At the same time it was held that the group had to follow a situationist course. Private ethics were clear, authoritative, and universally applicable: "Thou shalt not kill, steal, commit adultery, or give other personal offense." They covered every aspect of private moral choice: family, sex, work, property, relations with God and with other men. At the same time, the ethics of the group were never treated except in their relation to particular situations. In this sector of ethics it was understood that there were no absolutes. The group did not have to see things in black and white. It tried to make the best moral judgment it could in every circumstance. It did not have to go back to beginnings. The group's ethical choice was a blend of righteousness and expediency, always keeping an eye open to the outcome. These were the ethics of individualism.

Today the reverse is true—at least, among those under thirty or forty years of age. I offer it as the strongest proof that Western personality is becoming collectivized. An enormous number of our young adults feel that private ethics are situationist, and that public ethics are absolutist. They do not feel guilt—as the individualist does—for their private moral failings. But they feel an oppressive weight of guilt—as the individualist does not—for public failings. The great moral issues of their life are not the issues of private identity, such as work and sex. They are those of public identity, such as war and civil rights.

Much has been said about the younger generation's decline in morality. It has stressed their rejection of moral absolutes and their espousal of situation ethics. This is nonsense. While it is true that private moral sense is deplorably weak among many young people, they are intensely moral in their own way. In the public sector of morality they are as absolutist as their grandfathers were in the private sector. Furthermore, their guilt is harder to erase. The individualist can, of his own choice and by his own act, put an end to his sins. The collectivist cannot. He is not able, as a lone individual, to put away the sins he feels guilty for. He cannot, by himself, make a proper atonement. He feels a guilt that proves he is still capable of free choice, and therefore a person. But he is not an individual person in any moral sense, because he cannot feel guilt for his individual acts. Rather, he is only a part of a person. He is a participating member in a collective personality. Therefore he feels the weight only of group guilt. This is the factor that limits and defines his freedom and his accountability.

The current concern for the individual can be compared to the grin on Lewis Carroll's Cheshire Cat, which was still visible after the rest of the cat had faded away. Despite the individual's demise, however, there has been a strong effort to revive him. It has taken two forms, and each—ironically—has had the effect of steering him into collective identity. One form is socialism, and the other psychiatry. Socialism is the more obvious ploy. It is expressed in many ways, including communism, which sweeps the individual into a universal collective based upon class; and fascism, which enfolds him in a neo-tribal commune. A third way is the therapy group, which combines the collectivizing features of socialism *and* psychiatry. A fourth is the ecumenical movement, which seeks to gather the individual into a Coming Great Church.

Need for Transcendent Symbols

Behind all these remedies—and set at cross-purposes with most of them—stand the myths and symbols that used to give shape to Western identity. The failure, in our time, of these myths and symbols in no way reflects upon their reality. It merely reflects upon their present effectiveness. It is likely that the disappearance of these symbols is Western man's greatest loss. Even though he is beginning to adjust to a new, symbolless identity, a renewal in the vitality of his myths and symbols seems to be his greatest personal need. The symbolic wasteland that Western man has lived in for the past century has cost him dearly. It has led to personal emptiness, to futile mass movements, and to insensate wars. These conflicts and these movements have a different character than did those of the past. They are not brought about by the force of his identity and conviction, but by his lack of the same. Here is the reason for the feverishness of the era.

What are these myths and symbols that I speak of? The basic myth is an account of how God made man in His own image. This myth provides the necessary "historical" background for the symbol that derives from it—that man is like God. God has identity, and therefore man has identity. He is *idem*, the *same*. This myth has not been disproven. It has merely been set aside. It has been thrown into the discard by the behaviorists' argument that man as an individual is neither free nor responsible. Where this is taken at face value, men can only believe that the individual is *not* like God. Confronted with this logic, men can only take refuge in the possibility that the *group* is like God.

Another personal symbol is the threefold symbol of Christian baptism, in which the individual becomes a member of Christ, the child of God, and an heir to the kingdom of heaven. Behaviorism has put at least two of these to rest. Since a man can no longer be an individual, he can hardly have the child-Father relationship. As a person he is, and the Father may be, dead. Because his mind is now set in the mold of dialectical materialism, the individual can no longer think of himself as an heir to heaven's riches. He will have to be satisfied with being a member of Christ. This, at least, is plausible to one who has become a collectivist.

There is another kind of identity symbol that is available to man. It is the kind he has made for himself, such as the flag, the crown, the hammer and sickle. In the past such symbols have had a great effect upon the men whose loyalties they commanded. Today this is not the case. Even man-made symbols are being repudiated, for men are acquiring a new sense of identity that is not even shaped or influenced by symbols. This is a type of identity I have called *random-directed*, and which I shall describe in a later chapter.

How can we understand identity and all it involves? Some things we can agree upon. Identity requires a creative relationship between the individual and the group. This must originate with the group, which alone has the power to begin the process. To do this, however, the group must have a real life of its own. It must have myths and symbols to describe the culture and its origins. It must have values to give agreement, convictions to give vitality, and loyalties to bind men together. It must have functions to differentiate identity, as well as customs and traditions to guard it. Finally, there must be controls to regulate the individual, and an authority beyond the group.

The Key to Identity

The key concept in personhood is that of *identification*. The most important word, as it happens, is not a noun, but a verb—*identify*. Even this is most significant in an active and intransitive sense. We are not really what others identify us as being. *We are what we identify with.* As infants we had no identity at all. We had souls and bodies, but only a capacity for personality and conscience. Contrary to what some people think, personality and conscience are not givens. They were not there from the moment of conception. They were formed through our identifying with others and with what they thought, believed, and did. We copied them and drew upon those things that identified them, so that they could also identify us. We identified with our own and *then* we became individuals.

An Educational Fallacy

A real danger in the teaching theory of our day is the assumption that knowledge is pre-existent in the mind of a child. Because of this, the teacher is no longer a trainer, nor is he an authority. His job is to help the pupil find the answers within himself. Using the Socratic method (which Socrates labelled *maieutic* from the Greek word for *midwife*), the teacher helps the child to deliver his own idea, much as a nurse helps a mother deliver an infant.

There are things to be said for this technique.* But there is more to be said against it. At best it gives the child a sense of involvement in the educational process. But it encourages the child to see the ultimate as something within himself, and it casts the teacher in the role of a helper, rather than as a person who stands between the child and the subject matter.

This method's irrelevance to formal education becomes apparent when we realize that Socrates himself did not use if for this purpose. He used it not to give knowledge, but to teach the need for humility. He did not elicit an understanding his hearers could not possibly have. He asked questions in order that they could discover how little they really knew, and how poorly integrated was the information they had.

The damage done by this view of education has been the encouragement of a subjective view both of truth and of authority. The basic question in education used to be, "What does it mean?" Now it is a wholly different question, "What does it mean to me?" This novelty is at the heart of the teaching system that John Dewey introduced to America in the years between the two world wars. Progressive education was a concept that put authority in the eye of the beholder, rather than in the truth at which it looks. It was Dewey's way of propping up the individual. But what it did was to take away from the individual *and* the group the power to deal objectively with reality. Because of this, it brought to an end the possibility of giving identity through training. It acted on the supposition that the individual needed, at the very beginning, to be distinguished from the group.

The romantic idea behind Dewey's thinking was that the individual has within himself all of the elements needed for

* In support of this theory, many authorities who should know better have stated that *education* is derived from the 3rd conjugation Latin verb *ēduco, ēducere, ēduxi, ēductus*, meaning *lead out* or *draw out*. But in fact our word is derived from the 1st conjugation verb *educo, educare, educavi, educatus*, which means *train* or *teach*. This in itself suggests that education is not so much a process of drawing out as of putting in.

personhood. This is not only fallacious; it is dangerous nonsense. When this concept becomes universal it will, in a few decades, bring to an end the social character that man has laboriously built up over a thousand generations. This has not happened—yet—but there are signs that it is happening. The generation that was reared by John Dewey's maxims has shown history's first sharp break in identity.

There is a tremendous hazard in overidentifying with what is harmful, and in underidentifying with what is real and good. It is a hazard that is uniquely present in our time. This is so for the very reason that, in education, discipline is frowned upon and permissiveness is the rule. In the past, the nearly universal rule has been that of Proverbs, "Train up a child in the way that he should go, and when he is old he will not depart from it."* Permissiveness ignores the law of personality-formation, that the child needs and wants to identify with what is his, and with those who are supposed to be his own. If a child is discouraged from making such an identification, he will especially identify with the most gratifying substitute for what he really needs. This suggests that education requires more than a fuzzy kind of love and protectiveness. It requires discipline and training in the highest social wisdom.

Real training takes something that is unpopular in our day—prejudice and discrimination. In childhood, these things are not harmful to identity; rather, they are a necessity. The family into which the child is born must have made a prejudgment as to what is right for itself and the child. It must do what the child cannot do—discriminate. *Then* the child can identify. He can identify with what belongs to those who are his. This is no guarantee, of course, that he will. But it goes without saying that he will identify with what he is exposed to. He cannot identify with what he does not come in contact with. Training in the symbols and values of the group will assure that the child conforms to the standards of social personality. It

*Prov. 22:6 (AV)

assures that as an adult he will conform to the stance in which he was trained.

This is not all, of course. A true identity requires that one should have convictions as to what he must be *disidentified* with. This is the value of discrimination and prejudice—at least, of the life-supporting sort.

There are many things that are destructive to personhood. They provide the data for an ethic that must apply in all times and places. Yet such an ethic can be known only where real social personality exists. When its values are not self-evident, the group itself has to relearn, to the accompaniment of pain and suffering. Such a situation exists today in Scandinavia—one place where the life style I have called random-direction first became widely prevalant. It is a commonly accepted rule in Sweden that parents have no right to place a curfew upon their teen-age daughters, or to ask where they have been when they return from an all-night date.

Relation of Sex to Identity

Because sexuality is so important to personhood, Western man needs to be trained once more in its use. This applies not only to sex as such, but to the manly and womanly virtues that are such an important part of sexuality. In our time sex has ceased to be a function, and has become a role. Because of this the sexual virtues have disappeared. Sex has related only to the *persona* that people wear, and not to the inner identity that is intended to reflect the integrity of the divine. Sex is a role because the factory system has made it possible for women to forsake the functions that distinguished them for men. In working outside the home, they have been released from the ancient functions of wifehood and motherhood. These have become temporary roles, like masks that can be put on and taken off. The factory has made women independent of their husbands, so that men have lost the function of being providers and protectors. The factory culture has turned persons into interchangeable parts in a social assembly line. Women are no different from men. Youth and age are now one and the same. (If anything, wisdom and power belong to youth.) People have been homogenized into a condition in which sameness, rather than difference, is the mark of identity. The emancipation of women has led to the emancipation of the family. The home itself has lost its function. Because male and female are alike—in wants and needs and uses—sex has become unrelated to life. Breasts no longer belong to infants. Sex has ceased to be the source of life and a mark of identity.

The break between sex and life has been caused by Western man's loss in understanding of *function* and *differentiation*. But there is nothing that is real about his present assumptions. Every primitive society knows there is a differentiation in sexuality, and that it requires identity differences that extend to the very roots of one's being. It knows too that men can be allowed a far wider range of responses to sexuality than can women. This has nothing to do with justice or fair play; it is simply a fact of life. Women must have a pure sexuality for their children's sake, and for the sake of all children. At bottom, the laws of sexual conduct are not dictated by man's right to the pursuit of happiness, but by the needs of identity, which is the highest of all rights.

Nothing is more important than a satisfactory answer to the question, "Who am I?" There is an equally important question, however, that lies behind it, and that needs to be answered first, "Whose am I?" It is the uncertainty of this that lies behind the common childhood fear of adoption. Not only must every child have someone with whom he may identify. He must have someone with whom he is *idem, the same.*

Private Elements in Identity

There is a factor in personality that we have not yet touched. It is the internal factor of memory, imagination, and intention. These elements are the most powerful part of personality. Even though they are affected by training or by the lack of it, they are largely independent of environment. Memory, imagination, and intention belong to the seed and not to the soil. Their chief identification is with the soul—not with the culture.

The quality of our characters depends upon how well we integrate the symbols and standards of social personality with our memories, imaginations, and intentions. Our individual minds and wills are only by training related to social personality, but they are intimately and eternally related to the self. As such, they are relatively free from social control—even when this has been obtained through discipline and training. But their freedom is bought at a price. It is the price of corruptibility. Memory, imagination, and intention are the most vulnerable of all the elements in personhood. Their corruption in the individual is more damaging than the corrupting effects of society. This is because man-in-society can be trained, but man-in-himself can only be what he intends. If man's mind and will are not identified with the race's best vision of goodness and truth, he is not even a man. He is only a two-legged mammal—unique but not otherwise significant. This is why, of all the elements in social planning, training is the only one that is important. Training alone can effect the integration of individual and social personality. It alone offers the possibility of forming conscience, and allows man to identify with what is truly identifying.

Mysticism and Identification

At this point it will be helpful to think of identification as a form of mysticism. As we think of it, a mystic is a person who seeks to amplify his identity by seeming to lose it from time to time. His purpose, of course, is *identification with an "other"*—or, as social activists put it, *total involvement.* This can, however, be quite as destructive as creative. From a Judeo-Christian point of view, to identify totally with anything less than God Himself is idolatry. It is to identify with what cannot give life, and with what may very well destroy it. While there are kinds and degrees of identification, the only true mysticism is that in which the creaturely soul loses itself in the Soul of the Divine. The end of such an act is self-receiving—the restoration of a soul that is larger, wiser and more loving than before.

The Jews—who have the most ancient and unchanging form of social personality—have a singular rule. It forbids people under forty years of age to practice mysticism. The reason is simple yet profound. Mysticism can be dared only by those who already have well-integrated personalities. It is the most risky, as well as potentially the most creative, of personal activities. It offers a risk that youthful pot-smokers are woefully unready to take. It can properly be ventured only by those who have successfully identified with what, in the created order, is true and good. To identify with what is demoralizing and depersonalizing is to commit mental and spiritual suicide.

We see as a symptom of the West's identity crisis that men in the mass are practicing a debased form of mysticism. They are identifying with peoples and values and causes with which—aside from imagination and intention—they have nothing in common. The reason is twofold. First, they have such an anxiety about their own identities that they react against what is their own, and try to identify with what is not their own. Their hope is that in so doing they will be more acceptable to outsiders. Second, because men have accepted homogeneity as a good, they have come to believe there is more distinction in what is universal than in what is particular. They have opted, therefore, for what will erase identification rather than what will intensify it. The upshot in each case is that men overidentify with what is not basic. At the same time, they underidentify with what is appropriate and needful.

Misleading Folklore

There are two bits of folklore we would do well to dismiss. They reveal the contemporary anxiety about personhood. One is the saying that persons are more important than values. The other is the saying that real relationship requires us to accept uncritically the givenness of the other. Both are nonsense, for they assume that values can be separated from personality. They cannot. It is the possession of values, in fact, that gives identity. What is more, relationship can exist only where people can accept one another's values along with their persons. A Churchill can never identify with a Hitler.

The proof of a personal need for identifying values is this: A man can lose all the persons he loves and still keep his sanity, provided he is a well-integrated person. It is impossible, however, for him to lose his values without being disoriented in his identity. If his values have been real this amounts to insanity. One has, therefore, to have values to be identified. To renounce values for relationship's sake is to lose the ability to live responsibly.

Values in Apathy, Antipathy, Sympathy, Empathy

There is an insight to be gained from four words that have descended from the Greek *pathos.* They are *apathy, antipathy, sympathy* and *empathy. Pathos,* the word they have in common, refers to the feelings and affections. It touches especially upon the sufferings of human beings. As such, it is distinct from *ethos,* which refers to men's ability to help themselves. *Ethos* is active and impersonal. *Pathos* is passive, yet it elicits an active response because it is so intensely concerned with personhood.

At first glance, we might suppose that apathy and antipathy are negatively charged—that they are destructive to personhood. We might likewise suppose that sympathy and empathy are positive and creative. Such is not the case. Both apathy and empathy are negative because they are depersonalizing. Antipathy and sympathy are personalizing.

We all can understand that apathy destroys identity. It kills the other by acting as though he did not exist. What it also kills is the self. An apathetic person is in trouble. His stance is a symptom pointing to his own personal needs. Apathy is also a social, as well as an individual, trait. It can be seen in the caste life of India, where various social groups live in close juxtaposition without identifying with one another in any way.

Antipathy is not necessarily a negative. It rejects the

other's person, but it respects his personhood. The person who shows antipathy may hate and fear the other because he offers a threat. But he may also reject him because he has violated a standard that is essential to the integrity of both. In rejecting the other firmly and for good reason, antipathy leaves room for a change of heart. Antipathy may be the most creative way of bringing about reconciliation and fulfilment.

Empathy is intended to be positive, but it ends up by being a negative. To be sure, it is the very reverse of apathy. But it exaggerates the personhood of the other at the expense of the self. Empathy robs the self of the ability to be helpful to the other. The empathizing person overidentifies with the sufferer, and loses the power to be a source of strength and comfort. Not only does he fail in his endeavor to help the other, he loses the power to meet his own needs. Mystically, the empathizing person is leaning upon the one who needs to lean on *him*. He loses himself totally in the sufferings of the other. He loses his identity along with his power, and it will not—as in true mysticism—return. This is a depersonalizing stance. It keeps both parties from renewing their psychic power.

Sympathy is the one stance that is both positive and personal. It reaches out to others without depriving the self. The sympathizing person identifies with the other, but not to the point of having his own identity weakened. While he may refrain from giving all that the sufferer wants, he is willing to give all that the sufferer needs. In the process he himself is enabled to receive. In the act of identifying, his selfhood is not diminished, but enhanced. The sympathizing person does for the other what the other cannot do for himself; but he leaves it to the other to do what he can. This in itself is a therapy.

Flight to the East

A century-old phenomenon, widely noted but little understood, is the mystical flight to the East that has been joined by many of the West's intellectuals—and now by its young people. Here is the Pied Piper of Hamelin all over again. The trend has been a gradual one, but by now everyone can see it. It is discernible in our clothes and music, in our art and architecture—even in the mystical use of drugs. It is seen in our growing interest in the religious practices of the East, such as Baha'i and Zen, and the use of yoga.

This flight is *only* a flight, however, Whatever else they have to offer, the philosophies and religions of the East are unimpressive when it comes to the great issues of freedom and responsibility. Only Judaism and Christianity have ever handled these things well. Nevertheless, the flight is a fact. As a result, Western man has devalued his own best concepts of personhood. He is no longer free. He is no longer accountable to an authority that is external to himself. He is no longer engaged in a fruitful relationship with a personal Creator. His philosophy has become the pagan one of "accept and adjust." His religion is his response to the *within*.

One of the first Americans who embarked on this flight to the East was Walt Whitman. His poetry is both occidental and oriental. It shows curious ambivalences. In *Leaves of Grass* Whitman pictured democracy as "the guardian of personality, the nurse of individual . . . growth."[2] Yet in *Passage to India* he described that Asian subcontinent as "the historical cradle of humanity and religion . . . the symbol of spirituality and the ultimate meaning of existence."[3] Whitman's curious turn of mind is assessed by Emory Holloway,

> His long brooding on the surface phantasmagoria of life and nature had taught him the secret of sympathetic imagination, that "man is only interested in anything when he identifies himself with it," and that by such identification "the universal and fluid soul compounds within itself not only all good characters and heroes, but the distorted characters". . . and even the inanimate creation. This Oriental straying out of himself to dwell comprehendingly in the lives of others caused him to be "always conscious of myself as two."[4]

Whitman was an empathizing, rather than a sympathizing, person. He was among the first of a growing number of Americans whose identity-failure makes them want to be the other rather than to be themselves. Consequently, he identified so indiscriminately with *persons* that he lost the power to distinguish *values*. He projected himself into the distorted as well as the heroic. Religiously, Whitman was a pantheist. Perhaps this is why he looked to the East. He was a mystic who identified with the creature rather than with the Creator. Yet, despite his protestations of love for his fellow man, Whitman never identified with what was there by design—the pattern of manhood that is the image of God. Malcolm Cowley says this of him,

> In reality his affection was *not* for persons; it was rather for anonymous handclasps ... anonymous voices—integers, flesh, crowds ... even the wind and the water; anything but individuals.[5]

We need not touch upon his personal history. It is enough that Walt Whitman's universal and fluid soul was indiscriminating. It was as open to what did not belong to the self as to what did belong. Whitman never developed the power to reject; he had only the power to accept. As a result, he had a sense of personhood-without-function, and of identity-without-delineation. In this he was a prototype of today's common man. He was sensitive, identifying, open to others. But he lacked those traits that might single him out as unique, and as different from all others. Whitman identified to such a degree that his identity was impaired. His empathetic nature required a mystical draining of self. It created an emptiness that could not be replenished.

Symptomatic Crisis in Collective Identity

Whitman's plight is the plight of modern man. Here is the most pitiable of creatures—the man who can no longer be a real person because he is not sure of himself. This, of course, is the crisis of the West. It is a predicament that I have limned in simple strokes because I have only described the crisis' form. The form is clothed with a substance—which is emptiness and loneliness. Some of the confusion comes because the types of social personality are so violently mixed. A few people still have personality in the corporate sense, in which involvement is a good. Others are ruggedly individualistic. The majority, however, are collectivist. The trend is—and, barring an unforeseen and cataclysmic event, will continue to be—in that direction. Yet the triumph of collectivism, and the consequent simplifying of social personality, will be no victory for man. Collective personality, as I shall show, is always in crisis. Its anxiety is symptomatic, and will persist as long as the type continues.

In the years since the Civil War we have gone through a process very like one that happened in ancient Greece and Rome. There was a period then, as now, when the gods seemed to fail, and when philosophy took the place of religion. It was a time of insensate wars and cultural confusion. Now it is happening again, but with this difference. The disappearing gods of Greece and Rome never had been real. They were make-believe from the beginning. Today we are finding that even a real God can *seem* to disappear.

It is our science that has achieved this result. What the new philosophy has seemed to be saying, our science has overwhelmingly confirmed. It does not say there is no God, for it cannot. In fact, *physical* science is now supporting the Judeo-Christian postulate that God made all things out of nothing. But what *social* science is saying is that we are no longer free. What Pavlov proved with dogs we have now accepted as applying to ourselves.

It is fortunate that what man's mind tells him his heart rejects. Our sense of guilt is our own best proof of freedom. So is our sense of shame. Even symptomatic anxiety is a signboard pointing to human freedom. It says that liberty is something that is desirable above all else. It is our first prerequisite to personhood and identity.

We are not left without hope. What science has denied, religion has validated again and again. The lesson of Judaism and Christianity is that what man wants to be he ultimately becomes. The whole of human history is lined up in support of this thesis. The false understanding of this generation is thus overthrown by the living experience of every other generation. All we have to do, then, is to pay attention to that experience. All we require is to find our patterns of personhood in history, in preference to the other social sciences. History almost *has* to be the most creative social science, because it gives freedom and responsibility their due. Knowing this, we can accept a bit of illogic that must overthrow the best of logic: Man is free because he is a person, and he is a person because he is free. What man *is* even science cannot, for long, deny.

Notes on Chapter One:

1. Eugene Kincaid, "The Study of Something New in History," *The New Yorker*, October 26, 1957. The observer quoted is Major Clarence L. Anderson, an Army medical officer.

2. Quoted in *Walt Whitman*, by Henry Seidel Canby (Boston: Houghton-Mifflin, 1943), p. 268.

3. Quoted in *The Solitary Singer*, by Gay Wilson Allen (New York: Macmillan, 1955), p. 429.

4. Emory Holloway, *Whitman* (New York: Alfred A. Knopf, 1926), p. 115.

5. Malcolm Cowley, in an introduction to *The Complete Poetry of Walt Whitman* (Garden City, N.Y.: Garden City Books).

Chapter Two

THE RISE AND DECLINE
OF INDIVIDUALISM

From the beginning man has known that there is something unique about himself. He has the gift of self-consciousness. He has a sense of personhood. He feels a stamp of divinity that is not so evident in the world around him. He finds his uniqueness not in his bodily functions, feelings, and instincts—things he shares with his fellow creatures. His uniqueness lies in what the animals do not and cannot have. Because man alone possesses them, he may infer that they are *un*creaturely qualities. They *may*, in fact, describe the One who has made him. If this be the case, man may presume that he has as much in common with his Maker as he has with the creatures around him. He can believe that he is like God. Although he is necessarily a hybrid—in being both animal-like and godlike—he at least bears the stamp of divine personality. God has made him in His image.

While we are only too little aware of the uniqueness of the rest of creation, we can be sure of the uniqueness of man. We alone are, among the creatures, able to reflect, to plan and create, to act and to be responsible for what happens. Only we can detect the absolutes of truth, beauty, and goodness. Only we can know of an Absolute Person, of whom we are defaceable copies.

Distinctive Features of Man

We should not exaggerate the importance of self-consciousness. It did not unfold, in the way we usually think of it, until the ages of individualism. What distinguishes man as a species is not a self-consciousness that merely grows in him, but a few qualities that are his from the beginning. One is his ability to reason in the abstract. Another is his ability to adapt his environment to himself. A third gift is man's capacity for accumulating tradition. A fourth is his capacity for multiple associations. Like self-consciousness, this last is in primitive cultures only a possibility. It begins to describe man as his social complexity increases. It is, however, the most important single factor in the formation of individual personality.

Corporate Identity

With this as a preface, let us study the historical forms of personhood. Corporate identity is first. It is the earliest form—found in caste, clan, and tribe. Further, it is the only sure foundation for any form that may follow, whether in social or in individual life. This will take some explaining.

Until a few years ago, most Americans would have thought it absurd that anyone but an individual could be a person. Group personality would have been regarded as a metaphor. One might have cited the corporation, which is regarded as a legal person. The corporation can be said to be clothed with body, mind, and will. It has a life and a task, as does a man. It has differentiation of function. It has a system of communication and control. It has a need to present an agreeable "image" or *persona* both to its own members and to the world outside. In all these things it is "personal."

A simpler illustration of corporate personality might be the U. S. Marines, with their famed *esprit de corps*. This spirit, like the individual's, diffuses the body and brings it to life. Another example is the school spirit that descends upon a student body at a football game. In all of these illustrations group personality is more metaphorical than real. It takes cheer leaders, sergeants, and public relations men to bring such bodies to life. The members do not have enough in common to make them truly one—except on special occasions and in a particular way. What they have is *collective*—not *corporate*—personality.

The most striking claim to corporality is that of the *corporate state*. This term was used by the Fascists and the Nazis, who borrowed it from ancient Rome. It views the state as being something more than the sum of its citizens. The state is an organism with a life of its own. This life both includes and transcends the lives of the people. It includes all the generations of the past and the future. It is more, even, than these. The corporate state is viewed as an absolute. Its law is "the law of the Medes and Persians, which altereth not."* It is a body self-charged with divinity. While its government is not necessarily elected by its citizens, they are expected to identify with it totally. The government is their mystical embodiment. Its leader is their sacramental self. He is the "representative person" because he is the only one who is whole and perfect. Therefore he need not be accountable to the people. It is enough that he be accountable to himself.

Symbols of Identity

The distinction between corporate and collective personality can be seen most clearly in the symbols they use. The oldest and most popular of the collectivist symbols is the *fasces*, a bundle of rods bound together with an axe in the center. This was the symbol for leader and people in ancient Rome. It was used for a thousand years and more, beginning in the sixth century before Christ. Before it was associated with Fascism, the *fasces* was a popular symbol here. It was minted on the back of every ten cent piece. To Americans, as to the Romans, it meant, "In union there is strength."

The symbol of a corporality can only be that of a living thing. Whatever is to typify an organism must be an organism. It must suggest the functions and virtues and relationships that corporate life requires. Perhaps the best symbol we have is that of the Church as the body of

*Daniel 6:8 (AV)

Christ.* In this figure Jesus is the head, the Church is the body, and baptized people are the members.

There are other Christian symbols that are equally appropriate. One is that of the vine and the branches.† This figure suggests, even better than the body-symbol, what the Church's purpose is. Jesus is the vine; the disciples are the branches; the Father is the husbandman. The purpose of the organism is to bear fruit. This can happen only in a relationship where the branches are dependent upon the vine, and where the vine is dependent upon the husbandman. In this figure the disciples are called to bear fruit that can be identified as God's, and not as man's.

Two Concepts of Membership

The difference between corporate and collective personality can be illustrated in two meanings of the word *member*. The first is ancient. The second dates back only to the sixteenth century. Until the Reformation a *member* was considered to be a part of a living organism. Thus the finger, the eye, and the tongue were members of one body, as the root and the branch were members of another. In both the organism and the member there was total identification. The life of the organism was more basic, however, than that of the member. The member depended wholly upon the organism, and the organism depended only partly upon the member. To be "in the body" was essential to the very life of the member. It was essential only to the health of the organism. If the hand, for example, were cut off, the body would be disfigured but the hand itself would die.

With the rise of individualism this meaning became archaic—or at least it seemed to. A new, derivative meaning took its place. A member was now an individual who had voluntarily joined an association. The group itself was optional, so the individual did not derive his life or personhood from it. It could hardly define his functions or add

*1 Cor. 12:12-27; Eph. 1:22-3; 4:11-16; 5:23; Col. 1:18-24; 2:17,19; 3:15
†John 15:1-6

to his identity. The member could withdraw as freely as he had joined, and no one would be hurt. Neither he nor the abandoned association would have their integrity impaired.

The second of these meanings was virtually the only one used when the individual was the basic person in society. Membership was not vital to personhood. It was only of secondary importance in identifying a man. Even the Church was an aggregation of like-minded people. Now, however, a change is at hand. With the onset of collectivism, membership has once again taken on a vital significance. The group is a "person" once more. Togetherness is a vital mark of the new social personality.

This will not restore us, however, to the original concept of membership. A collective person is not a corporate person; even their symbols differ. What will happen is that membership will lose its voluntary quality. The individual will no longer be free. This is already true of the Communist Party, which requires total and permanent identification. It is happening elsewhere.

With this distinction, the three types of personhood begin to be seen clearly. Collectivism is shown up for what it is—a synthetic form of community. It attempts to create life where none exists. If there is a crowning type of personhood, it is in the independent individual. Yet even this form does not have to be. A tribe can get along without it. Corporate personality is paramount because it is most real, and most suited to the needs of men. It gives both life and orientation. It is found in biblical history, and in every simple culture. To get a broader understanding of it we must study the tribe. To understand it in our own experience, we need go no farther than the human home. Tribal personality is the kind first acquired by an infant. His entire world is the family fold.

The Tribal View

In the tribe the individual's view of himself is *only* that of a member. Whether his community be large or small, it is the only one he knows. He is totally identified with it, and cannot conceive of himself as having any identity apart from it. In such a setting, the basic person is the tribe itself. Governing all its members with a common set of traditions and customs, and of manners and morals, it provides a holistic and meaningful way of life. Tribal life is not fragmented and unrelated as is life in the West.

To say that tribal life is holistic, however, does not mean that it is undifferentiated. Age, sex, ability, and accomplishments give the individual more distinction in the tribe than they do in our more fluid and forgetful society. Unity is so natural to the life of the tribe that there is no need for the personal uniformity by which collectivists seek to recapture it.

There is another kind of uniformity that, to those seeking individuality, makes the tribe little more than a prison. It is the custom and tradition by which all tribal life is governed. The shackles of tradition allow very little innovation to the tribalist, and in this sense there is no freedom. The elaborate rules of tradition and custom that the fathers have given are, with the fathers themselves, the basis for tribal identity.

Formation of Conscience

Such is the background for corporate personality. Identity is formed by training, and is preserved by conscience and a sense of corporate justice. Here conscience is not regarded as a given. Tribalists do not assume, as did the youthful George Washington, that it is a spark of celestial fire. Conscience is implanted by the corporate person, not by God. It is society's means for assuring that the member will conform to the rules. It is imparted by drilling the child in the tribal values until those values will acquire their own authority—and will govern the member wherever he goes.

Another thing may be said about conscience. It is chiefly a negative rather than a positive force, which is why most of the rules must begin with the admonition, "Thou shalt not." Conscience does not take the place of reason. It cannot easily tell a man what he must do. But it can tell him what he must *not* do, and in this way it can help him find what the options are.

Corporate Justice

Corporate justice governs a culture only when its members have accepted the totality of their involvement. In the life of the tribe each member's actions affect the personhood of every other member. A transgression by one is an injury to all—just as a cut on the finger brings pain and impairment of function to the entire body. Because the offender is not yet an independent person he cannot hide. The hurt is quickly felt and the offender speedily detected. Punishment is swift; censure comes from all.

In the tribal setting the essential factor in member-control is that of *shame*. Shame is the essential part of punishment. Fear of shame is what keeps the offender in line. This has led sociologists to put the label "shame cultures" upon societies where the patterns of tribe, caste, and clan point to corporate personality. These are the cultures where *face* is important.

We cannot be surprised that men who have a corporate sense of identity should believe that they suffer for their *fathers'* sins—as well as for their brothers'. The law of cause and effect says this. Men have always suffered from and been blamed for the sins of those with whom they are identified. This is a fact of life. Furthermore, in a tribal society this not only *seems* just; it *is* just. Moses could not beg to differ when he heard God say:

> I the LORD thy God am a jealous God, visiting the iniquity of the fathers upon the children unto the third and fourth generation of them that hate me.*

It must be said, however, that Moses' concept of personhood was only corporate. The Law that he gave—insofar as it was not revised by later authorities—was corporate. The age of Old Testament individualism had not yet begun.

*Exod. 20:5 (AV)

Marks of Corporate Personality

One mark of corporate personality is the clannishness that allows the member to be at ease only when he is among his own. Outsiders can detect this quality in the *persona* or mask tribalists wear in the presence of strangers. American Indians, for example, put on an air of impassiveness. Children, when strangers are in their home, become stolid or shy.

Another mark of corporality is personal aggressiveness toward those within the fold. It is not so much an evidence of hostility as of responsibility. It is corporate conscience coming out into the open. Not all tribalists display this aggressiveness. Pacific islanders do not. It is seen among tribalists who are especially sensitive to outsiders. West African tribalists show this aggressiveness. They care greatly what their fellows do, because it affects the reputation of all. A similar aggressiveness is often a trait of American family life.

While the clannishness of tribalists is a sign of vitality, it is also a symptom of weakness. This was especially seen in the China and India that we used to know. Even though these were populous countries, and seemingly far removed from the primitive, tribalism remained the basis for personhood. Caste and clan protected social personality by providing invisible barriers against outsiders. In Africa, by contrast, the separation between tribes was geographic, and not social. In that continent corporalities kept their distance, as do animals, by having a territorial imperative. In Asia the separation was one of pretense. Thrown together geographically, the tribal units kept their distance by pretending that the others did not exist. Caste and clan adopted an apathy that simply ignored the other. When there was no acceptance of the other's personhood, moral obligation could be avoided. This explains why people in China and India could walk past the dying without even a glance of compassion.

Today, as for some centuries past, the only meaningful corporality in the West is found in the home. This is where the individual gets the roots of his identity. As he leaves the

family and becomes an entity in himself, he continues to
have need for corporality. There are many groups that
seem to offer this, but nearly all do so for the purpose of
exploiting him. The only real corporalities for later life are
the Church and the synagogue. Unfortunately, even they
are collectivist and exploitive in the way they are usually
run. There is only one other corporality that the adult
individual can discover. He finds it in establishing a home
of his own.

Causes of Individualism

We come now to the formation of individual personality. Historically, this happens when the tribalist finds
himself involved for the first time in a variety of *unrelated
associations.* The tribe becomes aware of a larger world,
and a few hardy souls venture out into it. These are the
men who may become individualists. The transformation
will not touch them all, of course. Some will return to the
tribal fold and resume the old identity. Others will be
captured and sold into slavery. Others will become brig-
ands, and exchange one tribe for another. Those who
remain in that larger world, however, and who become
involved and identified with its various groups, will indeed
become individualists. Only one thing is required; their
identification with other peoples must be voluntary,
honest, and responsible. This happens when tribesmen are
caught up in the life of trade, or in fighting distant wars, or
in migrating to new lands. The tribalist will find that he
becomes a person because his life now permits *disinvolvement* as well as *involvement.* He sees his identity delineated in his new mobility as well as in the old immobility.
In his self-identification he no longer thinks of himself as
being only a member. He no longer finds personhood in
total identification with one group. Because he is a member of several groups he cannot be totally accountable to
any. He can be totally identified with only one person—
himself. He can fairly be known and judged by no one but
himself.

When man is moving from tribalism to individualism

there is one quality that is prized even more than freedom. It is the sense of uniqueness that goes with multiple associations. The multiplying of associations means that men can develop a multitude of talents. Innovation and self-expression are not forbidden in an open society, as they are in the tribal prison. The new life means that everyone can be distinguishable—not merely the V.I.P.s. Membership in unrelated groups is its own guarantee that no two people can be alike. The genius that cannot even be unwrapped in the tribal cocoon can finally emerge. It can unfold, first as a semi-individual Chaucer, and finally as a fully individual Shakespeare.

Conscience in the Individualist

Looking back, we can see that there is one respect in which the individualist was never free. From the beginning to the end of the age he was bound by the tribal conscience. Even though that conscience was now trained in the individualist virtues, it was still a corporate device. *Social* personhood never came to an end. Training and discipline were even more strict than before, for now that the individual was intended to go free, it was more important than ever that he learn to conform. At this point, however, it was found that shame was no longer effective as a control, because shame is found only where the group is. In a free individual shame becomes obsolete. It is an emotion rarely felt, and is chiefly remembered as belonging to childhood. Fortunately, there was another emotion that took its place. It was the feeling of *guilt*. Guilt was the judgment of the absent group working on the erring individual. It was a form of government that—along with shame—could be instilled during childhood's corporality. Once the individual's conscience had been tested by his trainers, he could be allowed to go free. His own conscience could then become his prosecutor and judge. Man could be set free because, however much an individualist he became, his conscience never changed. Private conscience remained at one with the corporate conscience. Having such a conscience, the individual could be crea-

tively free from the old tribal involvement-with-persons.
He had the best compass there was.

There was a marked change in personality as man's
concept of self changed from that of membership in one
group to that of membership in many. None of a man's
groups could now make the demand of total involvement.
When all their expectations were added up, there was still
something left over. Separated from all his groups, he
found he could still act as a person. He thus began to enjoy
the things that go with private existence. He learned to
read, and became involved in a private world of ideas. He
became interested in puzzles and problems. He learned to
manipulate the shapes and forces of nature. This made him
more like God than before. At this point the individual
began to enjoy a private relationship with his Creator. As a
tribalist, his relationship with God had been possible only
by membership in the corporate Church. Now it was
one-to-One.

As it turned out, man had always had a symbol for such
a relationship. It was a figure that he had not thoroughly
understood until now—the Parable of the Good Shepherd.
Now he could see that he was one of God's sheep, and that
Christ was the Shepherd. Here the individual was still a
member—but a different kind of member. His dependence
upon the flock was not so great as when the flock had
been an organic body. The basic entities in this figure were
not the *flock* and Shepherd; they were the *sheep* and
Shepherd. The individual's safety lay in the Shepherd, and
not in the flock: if he wandered away from the flock, he
could still count on the Shepherd's attention. In fact, the
Shepherd had assured him that He had as much concern
for the one as for the ninety-nine.

Character and Values of Individualism

Individualism brought a change in social character as
well as in personality. The tribal virtues of loyalty and
solidarity lost some of their significance, and a new set of
virtues began to be preferred. These included initiative,
inventiveness, and self-sufficiency. They also included a

new mildness and a detachment that was possible only in one who did not share his personhood with those around him.

To be sure, the individual did not lose his corporate virtues altogether. His loyalty and his feelings of solidarity now involved the nation as well as his family and fellow townsmen. The tribal virtues had lost their priority, however. The nation was too large for its citizens to know one another and to keep the tribal sense of involvement. Nationalism, like individualism, came with multiple associations and with the new capacity for personal detachment.

The transfer of identity from tribe to nation did not affect the new individual's power to be himself. He was unawed by authority or bureaucratic involvement. His detachment gave him an extraordinary ability to deal with his own affairs. Unlike the later collectivist, he rarely empathized and had little concern for the image he seemed to convey. Nor was he apathetic, like the tribalist, to those he did not know. He could identify with anyone, without projecting himself more than would be helpful. His tools were sympathy and antipathy, and he used them very well.

One social trait is unnecessarily linked with the individualist form of identity. It is the so-called puritan ethic. Individualism's link with this "middle class morality" comes from the fact that, from the Renaissance on, those who devoted themselves to trade developed a mobility that made them highly individualistic. Despite this, the puritan ethic is not essential to individualism. The French and the English—both of whom have been individualistic—never adopted it. On the other hand, it is being used by people who make no pretense of individualism—the Russians and the Chinese. Its value is that, in a time of rapid population increase, it alone provides for the increase of wealth and of jobs that can prevent a decline in the standard of living. The value of industry, frugality, and thrift can be seen in a social context such as this. Industry maximizes production. Frugality minimizes consumption. Thrift converts the difference between consumption and production into job-creating capital.

Individual Justice

Unlike the concept of private personhood, individual justice is not hard to understand, and it needs no laborious development. In fact, it is the most elementary justice there is. Even a small child can understand it, as he makes a connection between his misbehavior and the punishment that follows. The truth is, a child has far more difficulty in understanding the corporate concept of justice. He sees nothing just in being punished for what his brother does. This concept does not even begin to make sense until one understands the rationale—as compared to the experience—of corporality.

Once a man has identified himself as a person in his own right, he no longer sees himself involved in his brother's ethical actions. The same is true in regard to his father. While he may suffer for his father's sins (as Moses said he would), he cannot be blamed for them. To the extent that he is at one with his father, he may even be a participant in his sins. But to the extent that he is disidentified from his father, he is free from blame. In such a case he is quite right in refusing to bear his father's guilt, or even to be a partaker in his shame. This is a point that needs to be made clear at a time when collectivists are using the burden of group guilt to add to people's demoralization.

The concept of individual justice was first proclaimed as a fact by the prophet Ezekiel. In 587 B.C.—some four hundred years after Israel had changed from a tribal to a monarchical form of government—he put an end to the force of corporate justice:

> The word of Yahweh was addressed to me as follows, 'Why do you keep repeating this proverb in the land of Israel:
>
> > The fathers have eaten unripe grapes;
> > and the children's teeth are set on edge?
>
> 'As I live—it is the Lord Yahweh who speaks—there will no longer be any reason to repeat this proverb in Israel. . . . The man who has sinned is the one who must die; a son is not to suffer for the sins of his father, nor a father for the sins of his

son. To the upright man his integrity will be credited, to the wicked his wickedness.'*

Another prophet, Jeremiah, had enunciated this principle a generation earlier—using, in fact, the same illustration. However, he had looked forward to individual justice as a *future* blessing:

> The days are coming, says the LORD, when . . . they shall no longer say, 'The fathers have eaten sour grapes, and the children's teeth are set on edge.' But . . . every one shall . . . die for his own sin; each man who eats sour grapes, his teeth shall be set on edge.†

Here is a most exalted idea of justice. It recognizes that justice deals with free beings, and that it must therefore be extended to the individual. It appreciates that corporate justice, to a large degree, is not even fair. (Corporate justice weighs a man down with guilt for sins that he has not participated in and may not approve of.) It apprehends that corporate guilt, if pushed too far, exacts a terrible cost to personhood. (The individual who is burdened with more than his share of group guilt can only be driven by the corporate mystique into surrendering what freedom and responsibility he has.) It intuits that even corporate justice cannot deal with the totality of evil. (There is a great deal of evil that God himself seems unable to deal with, short of a Deluge, and for which men would do well not to assume guilt feelings.)

The individualist idea of justice cannot deny the reality of corporate justice, because it cannot deny the reality of corporate personality. But it does assert the reality of the individual. Justice must deal with personhood at whatever level it exists. Individual justice has the advantage not only of a more perfect righting of wrongs, but of a more perfect unfolding of personality. In allowing a man to be free from the sins of his brother, it permits him to be more responsible for his own acts. In making him accountable for himself, it sets him as free as ever a man can be.

*Ezek. 18:1-3,20 (Jerusalem Bible)
†Jer. 31:27,29,30 (RSV)

Causes of Individualism's Decline

The rise of individualism is due to the interaction, in an increasingly complex culture, of men of faith. The two requirements are: multiple, unrelated relationships and faith—that is, *common* faith. So long as men believe in the absolutes that are given them, their personhood can blossom and bud. However, the time comes when the conditions for religion deteriorate, and when faith in the given is more than most men can possess. There comes a mingling not only of faith and nonfaith (which is found even in tribal society), but of faith and counterfaith. Men are daily confronted by others who have different ideas about God and the good—whose identity-symbols differ from their own. They may not want to identify with these people, but more and more they find themselves being identified with them. At this point the advantage of multiple relationships is cancelled out by the presence of multiple faiths. The old religion begins to fade, and philosophy steps in to take its place. Theism gives way, successively, to deism, agnosticism, and atheism. Men abandon their former gods and adopt new objects of worship. Whatever these be, it finally happens that man comes to arrogate authority to himself. In the process he acquires a wholly new concept of personhood. The old individuality has failed because man no longer has the psychic power to fulfil it. His values and symbols for a while were confused, but by now they have disappeared. Absolute purpose has been supplanted by agreed-upon goals, and intrinsic function has given way to role. As a result, personhood has been replaced by *persona*. The new personality does not come close to replacing the old, and man knows it. In his weakness of psyche, man seeks refuge in the group. He surrenders to it, in fact, and lets the group become The Group. The personhood it gives him in return, however, is not an intrinsic pattern. It is a man-made form of identity, with depreciated values and symbols. At the end of an age both of faith and individuality, man remakes himself in the small-scale image of what was.

The rise and fall of individualism is shown in the following projection. It takes Western man from the tribalism of the feudal period to the neo-tribalism of the twentieth century.

Age	Centuries	Philosophical and Religious Molds	Concept of Personhood
of Faith	10th, 11th, 12th	Medieval Synthesis	Corporate
of Hope	13th, 14th, 15th	New Learning, Renaissance	Transition to Individual
of Doubt	16th, 17th, 18th	Reformation, Enlightenment	Individual
of Despair	19th, 20th	Secular Humanism	Transition to Collective

Lest this seem to forecast an inexorable disintegration of personhood, we must remind ourselves of the truth of our basic assumption—that man is most himself when he is free and responsible. Even though the tides are running against *social* personality, the *individual's* identity is not ordained by fate. There never was a time when a man could not be a person. Men have always had an innate sense of the right, an innate desire for personhood, and an ability to study the lessons of history. It helps to know that identity is not found in a bureaucratic straitjacket or in a worldly abandon, but in the daily round of responsible living. It is reassuring to know that identity is formed more by what we identify *with* than by the way others identify us. It is promising to know that identity is formed by values as well as relationships, and that the dead contribute to it as well as the living. Above all, it is significant that identity is found in a God whose own personality all of man's best symbols and values reflect.

Chapter Three

THE NEW TRIBALISM

More than a hundred years ago, Europeans began to note in the Americans they met a type of social personality that had rarely been seen before. Americans were still individualists at that time, but they showed qualities that did not normally go with individualism. They had an affability and an attentiveness-to-others that brought instant appreciation. They were generous and expansive—hard to fault and quick to forgive.

This much was noted by Alexis de Tocqueville in his *Democracy in America*, published in 1835. A young Bostonian discovered this too. He was Richard Henry Dana, the author of *Two Years Before the Mast*. Dana recorded his astonishment at meeting in San Francisco a man whom he had know earlier as a severe and humorless New England deacon. In the West the man had undergone a transformation. He was uncritical, outgoing, friendly—an entirely different person.[1]

It was a type of personality that eventually became common throughout the country. When David Riesman wrote *The Lonely Crowd*—published in 1950—he described it as *other-directed*. He saw it as an orientation to people, rather than to values. As a type of social identity, he found it a refreshing change from the more inhibited types of *tradition-directed* (the corporate) and *inner-directed* (the individualist) personality.

Riesman's other-directed man was like the South Sea

islander, who was also kindly, generous, and alert to the moods of others. The American was not, like the Polynesian, a tribalist. But he was becoming—and by now has become—a neo-tribalist, whose life is centered in the people around him. The virtue of hospitality, which is common to both, is usually found where work is easy, the living comfortable, and the nation relatively free from threatening neighbors. This has always described Polynesia. Until World War II it also described the United States and Australia, whose people, by Riesman's standards, are the most other-directed people there are. Yet *their* closest neighbors, who have similar natural resources and the same isolation, are almost as inner-directed as ever. I refer to the Canadians and the New Zealanders. Why the difference? All four peoples came from the same cultural background, and have similar living situations. Why are two still individualist, and the others now collectivist?

Tradition and Social Identity

The answer is twofold. Australia and the United States have been more the melting pots, attracting a wider variety of peoples. As a result their values and symbols are the more confused, and their people now person- rather than value-oriented. The other reason is more basic. Those who emigrated to Canada and New Zealand were traditionalists, and intended to remain so, whereas those who went to America and Australia intended a break with tradition. As a consequence, Canadians and New Zealanders have remained individualists, while Americans and Australians have become collectivist.

The dividing line between the two types is tradition. Tradition is always present to the tribalist and the individualist. It is absent to the collectivist.* A century and a quarter ago, when Dana and de Tocqueville were making

*In making this distinction I use the word *tradition* to refer to *personifying values and symbols*, rather than to folkways. By this standard the Swedes are as collectivist as the Americans. The people of Sweden have kept their old folkways, but they have given up their personifying values and symbols.

their observations, they could easily have described the man they knew as "the winsome American." These traits were still visible at the close of World War II, when Riesman was making his observations. At that time Americans were being called from their previous isolation into becoming the champions of the free world. They shouldered a responsibility they had not sought—that of providing the policy, the arms, and the men to defend other peoples of the free-world community. Some traits could now be seen in Americans that had been true of them all along. The American had always been superficial. He was interested in everything, but not deeply committed to anything. What he wanted most was to be liked.

Other traits now came into view that had not even been there before. The American's friendly detachment was replaced with a new sense of interpersonal concern. Other people felt pressured into being involved with Americans, whether they liked it or not. In his new social personality the American was no longer sympathetic, but empathetic. He overidentified. To use Marshall McLuhan's terminology, he was no longer "cool" and "low-definition." He was "hot," and "high-definition." The philosophy of *responsible involvement* had made the American see the whole cosmos through "one world" spectacles. Even among his own people he could no longer be at ease or detached.

Polarization of Other-Direction

At this point, Riesman's other-directed man began to change. Other-direction itself began to polarize. It made a sharp break with the past, and became collectivist. The other-directed man whom Riesman had described was still, in many respects, an individualist freed from tradition. Now he had become a collectivist, and was diverging into two types. One was a neo-tribalist type, whom I shall continue to call *other-directed* (although in a narrower sense than Riesman used the term). The other is a neo-individualist type, whom I shall call *random-directed.*

Both as a political and as a personal form, neo-tribalism begins with an impulse that has been seen at many points in history. It never became universal, however, until the years after World War I, when chaos prevailed in Europe. At that time several neo-tribal societies sprang into being. Although their ideologies differed, their form was the same. Communism was neo-tribal in a "progressive" sense, while Fascism and Nazism were "reactionary." None was really inclusive, however. Each had its "ins" and its "outs." Furthermore, all had the same effect upon personhood: the individual had ceased to count.

Anxiety as a Sanction

We now turn to the neo-tribal man himself. What traits describe him? What is he like? First and foremost is his *anxiety*. This is more than a description; it is a means of control.

The need for anxiety is not hard to figure out. A collectivist society cannot allow either shame or guilt to regulate its members. These refer to values that find their authority outside the changing situation. In rejecting such authority, the society sets its own values—which, like itself, are ever subject to change. Now the only point of reference becomes the controlling group. At this point the individual is no longer permitted to be *value-oriented*—as in traditional societies. Rather, he must be *person-oriented*. The virtues that are now required of him are sensitivity and openness to others. His awareness and his deference to the group are proof of his will to conform. Only by being anxious for acceptance and approval can he be alert to what is required of him.

Aggressiveness

Another trait in neo-tribalism is *aggressiveness*. This is the same trait that we have noted in corporate personality. Like the tribalist, the other-directed man is *involved* with those around him. However, his is a different kind of involvement. The tribalist is aggressive only toward those who are his own—his family, his clan, and his tribe. He is aggressive with them because they share his personhood.

By contrast, the aggressiveness of the other-directed man is universal. It manifests itself in what, to the tribalist and the individualist, is an overweening *familiarity*.

Perfectionism

A third trait to note is *perfectionism*. This is as universal in neo-tribalism as is the anxiety drive itself. However, it is not something that originated with the neo-tribalist's sense of involvement. It belongs to the puritan ethic, which was programmed into the West's social identity at the time of the Reformation and has remained there ever since.

Along with this are three other traits that accompany the puritan ethic, and that tend to keep it in force. One is a *competitiveness* that requires every effort to be an improvement over what has been done before. Another is a relentless *judgmentalism* that will not allow mistakes. A third, which is an outgrowth of both, is *hyperactivity*. This last is seen in the compulsion to organize that is so characteristic of neo-tribal man. He suffers from the burden of others' sins as well as from his own, so he feels compelled to make his society better. He feels obliged to change his world by every possible means.

Homogenization of Society

A fourth trait in other-direction is the *homogenization* of the members of society. People tend to look, think, and act alike. As I have shown, this was a by-product of the factory system. The machine technology demanded operators who would be interchangeable and alike. They had to be both extensions and servants of the machine. However, in today's society it is not the workingmen who are the most homogenized. It is the owners of the machines, and those who use its products. The upper classes have borrowed the concept of personal homogenization.

In the early days of the Industrial Revolution there was tremendous opposition to the idea of piece-work. Fragmented tasks and round-the-clock shifts were unthinkable to men who had an organic view of life and work. As a result, the history of the labor movement was one of personal solidarity and resistance to change.

Even as late as the 1930s the laboring man was still largely tribal. He voted in a bloc. He was antipathetic to all but his own. Today, by contrast, he is more individualistic than his employer. He has acquired a private identity and his vote is his own. He joins with corporate-minded blacks in preferring segregation to the integration of the collectivist. He does not like the philosophy of involvement, and has as little as possible to do with intellectuals and social planners. He deeply resents the random-direction of the bourgeois collegians, whose education he must help pay for.

Two things have spared the former proletarian from the collectivism that so many others have adopted. One is the newness of his own individuality. The second is that the machine no longer makes its demands. The tasks that were so degrading have now been largely taken over by the machine itself. Many unskilled and homogenizing jobs have been automated. As a result, the factory worker has returned to the stature of a craftsman. He is no longer the machine's subordinate, but its master.

Meanwhile, for the rest of society the process of homogenization goes on. It is one that has especially affected women, who have been liberated from the tribalism of the home. Having developed multiple relationships, they have become individualists. For them, however—unlike the hardhat—the process has not stopped. They have been defeminized by a sexual revolution that is not so much one in morals as in function. As sexuality has become meaningless, women and men have tended to merge and blend in their personalities and character.

During the centuries of inner-direction only the men were really individualists. Only they could have a multiplicity of relationships. Even among them, individualism was limited to the upper and middle classes; workingmen were tribal still. But corporality applied mostly to women. Except for the rich and the gifted, women were restricted to the home. Their conduct was regulated by a sense of shame, and not—as with men—by guilt. Their individuality never quite unfolded as did that of men. But there was a profound social benefit in all this. It preserved corporality for society as a whole, and assured it for children.

Impersonality

A fifth trait in other-direction is *impersonality*. This is an outgrowth of tradition-rejection. When man turns away from the given in values and symbols, he can only identify with the group of the moment—and that by being anxiously sensitized to its members. He *has* to be impersonal; if he displays either the tribalist's emotional power or the individualist's convictions they will reject him. He can only profess himself in a *bland awareness*. He can only express a desire for "deep" and "meaningful" relationships.

Fear of the Future

The final trait of neo-tribalism is *fear of the future*. Because the collectivist cannot rise to great personal heights, he must lean upon the group for identity and direction. In so doing, he must surrender the individualist's forms of government, which are the monarchy and the republic. These look to the past. They give heed to the absolute—in symbol, value, and authority. Because they can do this in faith, individualist governments can face the future with relatively little apprehension. On the other hand, the neo-tribal government—whether in the final stages of democracy or in dictatorship—can only be the expression of an already-collectivized social personality. It is intended not to liberate man *for* the future, but to protect him *from* the future. It is an insurance policy to cover the neo-tribalist's loss of faith in himself and in his past.

Social Props for the Individual

I have spoken of socialism and psychiatry as supports for men when the old order begins to fail. Both are products of the philosophy that springs to life when faith in a personal God is lost. Socialism is its own authority for setting aside earlier forms of political economy, and for supplanting them with new forms. Psychiatry is its own authority for experimenting with new forms of person-hood.

This is not to be critical of these things as expedients, granting the premises on which they are based. Psychiatry is a necessity in the final stages of inner-direction, because private personhood has a weakness that does not exist in tribal life; it is the individual's difficulty in being absolved from guilt. In the tribal state, the ire of the group is quickly aroused against an offender. Since his self-image is entirely dependent upon acceptance with his fellows, he must face up to what he has done. He must make an open confession, with restitution and promise of amendment. Once he has humbled himself he can be absolved and restored. The experience is therapeutic, both for the indi-vidual and the group.

In an individualist society no such benefit can be found. Once a person has left the corporate group, there is no one to whom he can make a confession. This is why the Protestants had to institute confession directly to God. Protestant religion gave the individualist an unfailing cor-porality and a Person to be absolved by. But as God and personhood lost their meaning, even this lost its power. By now men were half agnostic, and they got no sense of release or restoration. Especially where the puritan ethic was in force, their sense of guilt became increasingly op-pressive.

Psychiatry gave new hope to broken individuals. It pro-vided a new point of reference, and gave a sense of release. It created a kind of corporality for those who had never had one. It offered a father-figure with whom the patient might identify—the therapist. It offered a mother-figure— the therapy group. This meant that the patient was no longer alone. He was acceptable to some others, and he could once more accept himself.

Social Costs of Psychiatry

There was a drawback to this, however. It applied both to private and social identity. Psychiatry tended to restore the patient's self-esteem at the expense of real individuality. It healed him by making him a collectivist. The therapist reduced his guilt by taking away some of the standards and values that caused it; he also convinced him that his sins were not really sins, but only mistakes. Moreover, they were not to be blamed upon him so much as upon those who had influenced his life. The patient's sense of responsibility was thereby reduced by permitting him to think of himself as conditioned—not really free.

In saying this to its patients, however, psychiatry said it also to society. It taught man to forget the old idea of sin, and to disregard the old constants. The individual was encouraged to give up the attempt to navigate on his own, as it were—setting his course by the sun and the stars. He needed no longer depend upon the heavenly absolutes. Instead he was supposed to guide himself, as do ships in a wartime convoy, by orienting himself to those around him. Applied to society, this concept had one drawback. While it assured safety from collision, it offered no assurance that the entire convoy would not run aground. Moreover, it offered no way to reach the goal to which only celestial navigation could be a guide.

Psychiatry weakened the group even while it was healing individuals. It attended to men at the expense of man. For the sake of healing, it had to pretend there were no absolutes. What it also failed to note was the character of society's controls. Shame and guilt had been oriented to morality, and had pointed to the reality of social character; but not so anxiety. In steering man from a weakened individualism to a neo-tribalism, the psychological sciences were engaged in an immorality of their own. They were concerned only with the few and only with the present. They left it up to the sociologists and statesmen to deal with the many and with the future. Sigmund Freud was quite frank about this:

> We have found it impossible to give our support to conventional morality (which) demands more sacrifices than it is worth. . . . If after (our patients) have become independent by the effects of the treatment they choose some intermediate

course . . . our conscience is not burdened whatever the outcome.[2]

Training in Collective Identity

So far we have touched only upon the ways in which
society has accidentally stumbled into other-direction. We
may now consider how its members are being trained in
that direction. The most important is John Dewey's progressive education. This technique is *pupil-centered*—as opposed to *content-centered*. That is, it emphasizes persons
rather than values. It focusses upon the child and his
capacities rather than upon the learning material. It tries to
capture the child's interest, rather than train him in a
discipline. If the child loses interest (or fails to see the
relevance) the study is dropped. The child is not made to
do anything, and the demands of external reality are not
pressed upon him. Because progressive education discour-
ages hierarchical leadership, the child becomes his own
leader. He is encouraged to view all knowledge in subjective rather than objective terms.

Meanwhile, the home has given an impulse of its own to
other-direction. While the schools were failing in authority
and discipline, the family was failing in acceptance. Infants
could not find the consistent examples of love and authority that they needed. After a few drinks their fathers often
changed frighteningly. Mothers made it clear, in using
sitters, where their hearts were. Furthermore, as children
grew up they got no clear idea as to whether their parents
believed in anything. Parents seemed only to want their
children to be popular—and to accept their parents as
equals. The youngsters did not want this. They tried to
make their parents give them discipline. They resorted to
rebellion and delinquency in order to find what the
bounds of behavior were. Their parents' response was only
fright and uncertainty. This increased, rather than eased,
the children's confusion. More and more, as anxiety
abounded, social personality seemed to require what Dewey was pointing to—adjustment to people, rather than to
what was thought to be unchanging.

Group Dynamics

Shortly after World War II a technique was found for training adults. It is called *group dynamics*, and is like progressive education in purpose and method. Psychologists had discovered that adults as well as children learned more readily by activity and discussion than by listening to lectures. Group dynamics was a training technique based upon this discovery. It brings adults together in *sensitivity-* and *leadership-training institutes*, where the findings of psychology can be demonstrated and shared. There, through role plays, discussion, and behavior analysis, adults are sensitized to the feelings of others. *Training* (or *T-*) *groups* give a simulation of real-life situations, with all their ambivalences. They give practice in leadership skills—especially in the illusion of shared leadership. In the process, participants discover new insights into their own natures, and into the nature and needs of the group. By being artificially freed from the inhibiting of feelings, members are able to develop—at least temporarily—a high degree of mutual trust. Their openness allows the submission of feelings and opinions—and their gracious acceptance as well.

During the past few years group dynamics has been used as a training device for all sorts of organizations. Its effect has been to restore to participants some of the unstructured corporality they have enjoyed in earlier life. As T-group experience has filtered through industrial organizations it has been discovered that even in business, leadership can be shared. The concept of the unstructured committee is an exciting new breakthrough. The virtues uncovered by group dynamics are those that inner-directed people tend to need and that other-directed people tend to have: candor, openness to others, willingness to express personal feelings, sensitivity to the feelings of others. T-group members whose own personalities are in transition from inner- to other-direction have found the experience therapeutic as well as instructive. It has enabled them to be rid of the guilt and anxiety feelings that are not easily sloughed off in the more guarded relationships of everyday life.

For true individualists, however, the T-group is a traumatic experience. Many of its "real-life" situations are all too real. They make the group-at-hand become the only group. They make the group's—or rather, the trainer's—authority become the only authority. When the trainer stays in the background—as he is supposed to do—the real happening is undetected. It is a subtle change in the group's members from individual to collective personality. On the other hand, when the trainer becomes impatient and shows *his* feelings, he is likely to become savage in his attempt to destroy the members' individuality. The result can be horrifying. The group has been forbidden to structure itself, and to permit a natural leadership to emerge. Consequently, it can only accept the trainer as *Der Fuehrer*. Anything else is contrary to the givenness of the training situation. The individual cannot stand up against the trainer, nor can he expect to find allies. This is a fact that, so far, has been neglected by the exponents of group dynamics. It offers a baleful prognosis for the future of group life.

Experiences such as this tell us that the ability of multiple associations to give individuality is being wiped out by the homogenizing of our groups themselves. Increasingly in our world we are unable to *have* unrelated associations. Having lost a sense of form and function, each of our groups is becoming like the other. Groups as well as individuals are now unstructured. Differentiation is looked upon as an accident. Consequently, the fifteenth century's Everyman is being replaced by the twentieth century's Everygroup.

Group dynamics is a helpful art to know. Put to work in the cause of collectivism, however, it can be demonic in its effect. Those who are in the T-group can hardly sense the purpose of their training. The whole process is too nearly subconscious. As time goes on, the real—if unconscious—purpose of group dynamics begins to emerge. It squeezes adults into the same mold that Dewey pressed children into—the mold of collective personality. The ethics of such a use are highly questionable. For the first time it is possible to change people's social personality without their knowledge or consent.

Let us now see what the options really are. Other-direction is sought because of its supposed virtues: sensitivity, openness, facility in communication. Yet this is not achieved. The other-directed man's sensitivity is cancelled out by the neo-tribalist's aggressive involvement. The other-directed man's honesty and openness are cancelled out by the neo-tribalist's anxiety about his public image. The net result is one of loss. For proof of this we have only to look back to the 1930s. At that time, the neo-tribalist's traits of blandness, agnosticism, perfectionism and aggressiveness took on their most menacing hue. Virtually the entire German lower middle class became Nazi. In doing so, they reverted to the mythical symbols and irrational values of a collectivist "blood and soil."

The neo-individualism of what we once called the under-thirty generation is a protest against this form of person-hood. It is a protest in behalf of the virtues that got lost in the shuffle—honesty, sincerity, and sensitivity. Before we consider the significance of random-direction, however, let us orient ourselves to the world as we know it today—or at least to the world as we knew it ten years ago. I shall confine myself chiefly to the West.

Social Identity in the U.S.A.

In our own country other-direction has been, for several generations, the identity form of the northern, urban, Protestant middle class. Today virtually all middle and upper income Americans are other-directed, *except for those under thirty-five or forty.* Inner-direction is chiefly found in the South. Elsewhere it is found in small towns and rural areas, and among middle income black people. It is found among the fundamentalist Protestants, many of whom are the workingmen already referred to. It is also found—at long last—in Catholicism. This is due to the Roman Church's relaxation of the corporality to which the

Counter-Reformation held it. It is due also to the discovery of his own individuality by the Catholic workingman. Corporate personality is found in the family life of Catholics and of inner-directed Protestants. It is found in a few ethnic groups, such as Mexicans and Puerto Ricans. It is eagerly sought by black Americans, whose greatest frustration has been their inability to acquire it.*

Social Identity in Europe

The social identity of Europe is mixed, much as it is in America. The Catholic south is still largely corporate. This is the result of a historical accident, in which a cycle of personhood was reversed. There was a time when southern Europe was, if anything, more individualistic than the north. What destroyed individualism in the south was the Reformation in the north. A broken Church had to be healed. When the Reformation came, most of northern Europe became Protestant and adopted the concepts and ethics of individualism. The Counter-Reformation rolled the rest of Catholic Europe back into corporality. This did not mean that multiple associations came to an end. They just were not allowed to count. The Church kept within its grasp most of the forces that identify and personify the individual. Only recently—with Vatican II—has this authority been relaxed. Only now has the authority of *unrelated* associations been allowed to assert itself.

In the north, by contrast, inner- and other-direction are prevalent. Individualism is still found in Britain and in

---

*Since our recent civil rights legislation has begun to bring white Americans' compression of blacks to an end, and with the blacks' own migrations to northern cities, negroes have had an increasingly weak self-image. The desire for corporality lies behind many of the black movements of the day—black power, black nationalism, black studies, black cultural exchanges, and even a black mythology. As attempts to satisfy unfilled psychic needs, these point more in the direction of collective than of corporate identity. Yet in keeping emphasis on blackness, they protect negroes from the vague undifferentiation of other-direction. And in giving blacks the experience of multiple associations within their own institutions, they permit the development of what other ethnic groups today possess—a fairly rugged individualism.

parts of France, Switzerland, and the Low Countries. Northern Germany and Scandinavia, which *were* individualist, became collectivist some decades ago—although West Germany reverted to individualism in the years after the war. Poland and the Balkan countries are still largely Catholic and group-oriented. There and in Russia the conflict is between corporality and collectivism; individualism has seldom been an issue.

The cause for collective identity in Germany and Scandinavia lies in the past nature of the Lutheran Church. Like the Anglican, it has been a state church. Its support came from the middle and upper classes. It did not identify with the workers and peasants, and they did not identify with it. Consequently, a hundred or more years ago the workers and peasants were atheists. Their disbelief infected the populace. They were ready for Marx—even though they had to export their revolution to Russia to make it succeed.

The poor of Britain, by contrast, were saved from collectivism by the Wesleyan movement. So were the poor in America. The English lower classes, like ours, won their power with votes—and not with guns. John Wesley converted the poor to the puritan ethic and to individualism with promises that could be made good here as well as in heaven,

> We ought not to prevent people from being diligent and frugal; we must exhort all Christians to gain all they can, and to save all they can; that is, in effect, to grow rich.[3]

Today, however, nearly all of Europe is neo-tribalist. Even where tradition still persists, change is coming fast. It can be seen in the way people behave. They are "hot" and "high definition." They are more interested in winning than in playing the game. Their business life is competitive. They are deeply concerned about the future. In their shops and on the highways they are pushy and assertive. They identify quickly with strangers—showing a familiarity and a curiosity that are quite novel. Even their news media disallow privacy.

Only in Britain is there much evidence of a sense of detachment. The British still have a modesty in interpersonal relations and a willingness to live and let live. Personhood is not yet shared.* Traffic is orderly and rules are respected. People line up in queues. Perhaps this is why Asians and Africans continue to flock to England to pursue their studies. These people are no longer tribalists. They are inner-directed too. Reading and travel have, in a generation or two, done that much for them. Like the English, these Africans and Asians treasure the virtues of politeness and reserve. They are not comfortable with Americans and continentals, who are all too familiar. These Asians and Africans, newly released from the bonds of tribalism, can more readily identify with those who are also "cool" and "low definition." They respect the difference between the English and themselves, but they value the similarity.

Causes of Transition

Three events provide the key to Western man's transition. They tell us why he abandoned his individualism and became a collectivist. Before these events took place there had been confusion. There had been a mixture of faiths and symbols. The events destroyed the symbols themselves—and therefore destroyed the faiths. One was Darwin's discovery of *physical* evolution. Another was Marx's doctrine of *social* evolution. The third was Freud's theory of *mental* evolution. Each stripped away a part of the veneer that covers the hidden. They pried under the conscious mind of man (the part that deals with facts and values) to reveal the subconscious mind (the part that deals with myths and symbols). They opened Pandora's box and brought to light the things that do not stand exposure. As man's myths and symbols were revealed in all their dimensions, they dessicated and crumbled. Both symbol and identity went down the drain. Darwin seemed to be saying

---

*This remains true, I believe, of the Calvinist portions of the Continent, especially in Switzerland and Holland, where geography as well as history has allowed detachment.

that man was not, and never had been, made in the image of God. He was only a naked ape. Marx declared that there never had been a God; man could not, therefore, be His child. Freud went still farther. By showing the destructive potential in sex and family life, he turned a primal function into a questionable role. In reducing fatherhood to ashes, he upset the grandest relationship that had existed between God and man.

If we would look for a turning point in the transition from individualism to collective personality, it can be found at a time when America was on the brink of the Civil War. 1859 was the year in which Charles Darwin published his work, *On the Origin of Species*. In that same year Karl Marx published his *Critique of Political Economy*—later to be enlarged and rewritten as *Das Kapital*. These two traced out a sketch of a mechanical man in a mechanical universe.

It remained, of course, for Freud to make the largest contribution of all. That contribution—and the completing of the picture—did not come until another generation had come and gone. In 1859 Sigmund Freud was barely three years old.

Notes on Chapter Three:

1. Richard Henry Dana, *Two Years Before the Mast* (Boston: Houghton-Mifflin, 1911), p. 467.

2. Sigmund Freud in a paper, *Formations Regarding the Two Principles of Mental Functioning* (1911), quoted in a foreword by O. Herbert Mowrer to William Glasser's *Reality Therapy, A New Approach to Psychiatry* (New York: Harper & Row, 1965), p. xix.

3. Quoted in Max Weber, *The Protestant Ethic and the Spirit of Capitalism* (London: George Allen & Unwin, 1930), p. 175.

Chapter Four

THE NEW INDIVIDUALISM

For many years random-direction was only the mood of an avant-garde. It was the type of identity found in a tiny company — the artists and writers who sense a turning point before others do. These men had seen the ugliness and despair of contemporary life, and sought to lay bare the truth. For decades they were merely voices in the wilderness, to be laughed at or ignored. By the 1960s, however, the avant-garde was finally vindicated. The identity form to which they had pointed finally appeared on the scene.

Despite its novelty for most of us, random-direction is not a new form of identity. As a type of social personality it attended the declining years of Rome. As a type of individual personality it has always been seen in a small minority. It has been the identity form of the nonconformist and the criminal.

Random-direction makes an island of every man. It gives him total autonomy. It denies the force of tradition, custom, and all that bears witness to a given authority and morality. It is opposed to every institution. Apart from the responsibility of men to protect selves, it acknowledges no other law. Random-direction is anarchic. It seeks the same state as that of animals in the wild, doing what comes naturally.

David Riesman has held that inner-direction is not to be equated with morality. He says that an individual in an inner-directed society can set up private goals that may be contrary to those of the group.[1] I believe such a person would be not inner- but random-directed. Individualism, like tribalism, has the intention of fulfilling tradition and custom. It is only the antisocial member of these cultures who does not have this intention. He rejects the controls that society gives, and never develops a conscience.

Emergence as a Social *Form of Identity*

It is not hard to see why criminals are random-directed. They have no responsible involvement. They reject the authority of society, and set their own standards and goals. Now, however, random-direction has emerged as a type of social personality. The old perspective is dissolving, and a new one is beginning to focus. Random-direction is a category that includes people of good will as well as those of ill will. It includes those who have the intention of being responsible. This offers a new possibility—that a society of anarchists *might* be an ordered society. Even though it had an element of criminals, it would have a majority who valued the rights of others, and who were capable of unselfish relationships. The critical point for such a society would be the point of transition from other- to random-direction. Unlike criminals, who are most prosperous in an institutional framework, random-directed people of *good* will might be compelled, for the sake of their morality, to destroy every institution and custom.

Origins in Rebellion

As a type of social personality, random-direction takes its origin in protest. It is the rebellion—seen today in the young and the thoughtful—against the timidity, the conformity and the hypocrisy of those who have run the world. Like all protest, the youngsters' is partly for and partly against a number of things. They are against their parents and against the Establishment, and against the demands both make. They are against the *given*, which only limits their freedom. What they are for is life at least, as they understand it. They feel no obligation to living or dead. They want only to set man free.

Random-direction has coalesced with startling rapidity from a mood to a form of identity. This has happened in the past ten years. What is more, it has occurred in three different milieux. One is a rebellion against a still-puritan collectivism. Another is a reaction against an inner-direction that is in a phase of decline. The third is a revolt against a degrading tribalism. Each is the rebellion of the young people against an unacceptable older order.

The first is the revolt of American whites and of many Europeans, who reject the ambivalence of neo-tribalism. The hypocrisy they abhor is what John Dewey spoke of forty years ago:

> The combination in the same person of an intensely executive nature with a love of popular approval is bound . . . to produce what the critical call hypocrisy.[2]

A similar revolt is going on in England. In the years since 1960 many young Britons have been rebelling against the decadence of the inner-direction they find in their elders. Youngsters from upper-class homes reject the hypocrisy of parents who accept the symbols of tradition without practicing its morality. Youngsters from middle-class homes reject the hypocrisy of parents who accept the morality of tradition without professing its symbols.

At the same time there has been, on this side of the Atlantic, a rebellion of young, urban negroes against the timidity and conformity of their parents—most of whom were shaped by the tribal society of the black south. The differences among the three are minor, and lie chiefly in the nature of what is being resisted. The American whites are reacting against the puritanism of their neo-tribal elders. Their chief concern is with identity. The English are concerned with the hypocrisy of accepting value on its own authority. They have no tie to religion, and want to enjoy themselves. The black youth's rebellion is against Whitey and against his own Uncle Tom. He is therefore more inclined to violence. He must fill in what has been lacking in the aggressiveness of black corporality.

Although all three are presently random-directed, there is one important difference of intent between the blacks and the whites. The blacks are fighting for a real tribalism. They feel the need to draw a line between their own and those on the outside. They are bitter against the whites for having broken up their corporality. They are resentful of middle-class blacks for their seeming lack of concern for black solidarity. The white youngsters, by contrast, want only to be let alone. They are neo-isolationists. While they feel a bond with others who are random-directed, they deny all other links. They value the detachment of having an independent self.

Random-direction is always opposed to tradition. Other types of social personality have not been. Tribal and individual identity depend upon tradition, and neo-tribalists are afraid to let it go. The latter begin to part with tradition, however, by surrendering its myths and symbols. They lose sight of the connection between the symbol (as given by God) and the ethic (as an expression of the symbol). They treasure the ethic as though *it* were their god. Random-direction recognizes the fallacy, if not the hypocrisy, of such thinking. It throws both symbol and ethic out the window. Traditional values are finally recognized for what they are—nothing at all if not associated with a Giver. Random-direction thus becomes the first and only type of identity to make a decisive break with the past. This is its nature and, to some degree, its worth.

How did the rebellion come about? I speak, for the moment, about that in America, and especially on our campuses. It can hardly have been directed against the man that Dana and Riesman had described. He was not that obtuse. His character did not invite rebellion. His openness and sensitivity would, in fact, seem to be the very qualities that young people would wish to emulate. What happened was that, in the years after World War II, other-direction was polarized and these qualities were lost. America was thrown into a cold-war world, and its citizen lost his "cool." His country had to forsake its isolationism, and become involved in a neo-tribal liaison with many other nations. It was, in fact, the keystone of that confederation.

The whole system of security hung upon the reliability of the United States. This gave the American a responsibility he had never had before, and did not especially want. As his country gave up its gracious detachment, so did he. As it became aggressively involved with others, so did he. As the coalition became concerned with power and face, so did he. The new *persona* was a form of hypocrisy he could not get away from. It drew the expected reaction from behind the Iron Curtain. But it also drew a reaction from those he had hoped were his. Polarization did unpleasant things to him, and the youngsters' eyes were opened. They discovered that their fathers' virtues had not been virtues after all. Their tolerance was not a loving acceptance of differences; it was merely a want of convictions. Their tact was not a respect for the feelings of others, but only a consulting of fears.

Childhood Roots of Random-Direction

Before touching the personality traits of random-direction, let us consider the way the young people were reared. This was the first generation to have been brought up without any discipline. It was the first to have been reared in an environment that treated the home and the school as a single unit. That scheme did not even give to adults the benefit of multiple relationships. The teachers governed the family through the P.T.A. The parents, in return, limited the teachers' authority by forbidding the rod. There was a new absolute that no one could touch the child.

Two things disappeared along with childhood discipline. Authority lost all its meaning. Reality became more subjective than ever. Because they had not been touched by these things, children could find no clearly etched limits to their own identity. As a result, when the children got to college they had the healthiest bodies and the most poorly nourished minds on record. No one had ever said "No" to them. They had never learned to say "No" to themselves. Mistaking their shallow projections for reality itself, they resorted to childish methods to get what they wanted. Their thing was the campus-wide tantrum. The proof to them of their rightness was this: when they began as a group to throw their weight around, society's response was the same as their parents' had been. It was the response of timidity, anxiety, and irrational guilt. Their confrontation meant little, however. They were never able to discover authority. They had to keep testing the bounds of behavior.

This, of course, is a simplification. I justify it only because we are concerned with personhood—and not with social issues. It does, however, set a few props in place, so that we may look at the other side of the scene. That side is the home—the place where children's needs have been met in the past. This, unfortunately, is no longer the case. Not only have parents been depersonalized by the over-throw of function. The home itself is no longer the de-tached entity that it needs to be. It is no longer tribal, it is merely neo-tribal. Because parents have bought the philos-ophy of involvement, the home has been blended with the rest of the world. The hot tempo of other-direction reaches inside the home, destroying its coolness and de-tachment. It is no longer "low-definition"; rather it is "high." It is inclusive rather than exclusive. Even its archi-tecture exposes it to the world. The demands of outside institutions reach into the home so that *it*, in effect, is an extension of *them*. Alien groups thus involve themselves with the family members, and separate them from one another. Even the incessant bombardment of media reaches into the home, disrupting and perverting its func-tion. The home is no longer a haven of blessing and peace. It is a logistical center—a machine for living. It cannot offer its members a needed disinvolvement from the world.

Personality Traits

We shall now consider the personality traits of random-direction. Many of these it has inherited from other-direc-tion. At least, this is so in the puritan countries, where there has been a state of other-directedness. The remaining traits it has evolved on its own. As with other-direction, random-direction is humanist and subjective in its view of reality. Its main tradition is the idea of personal homo-geneity, inherited from the industrial revolution. It is embarrassed by ·differences in heritage, such as race, class, or nation. It sees no value in functional differences, such as the sexual and parental. It rejects the relevance of the religious differences that are based upon fixed relation or value. Such differences are viewed as unfortunate discrepancies. They are an offense to the personhood of random-direction. They are unholy, and have to be blended or erased. Yet, because homogeneity is in itself a threat to individuality, one ultimate distinction must be admitted. It is the distinction among entities. Each individual has the right to be a person, and is therefore both separate and sacred.

Aside from the values of the machine age there can be no real tradition. Social personality is no longer even thought of as a possibility. Identity, by definition and intention, can only be individual. Therefore there are no lessons to be learned. One person's experience cannot possibly be helpful to another—unless in the therapy-rite of show and tell. For this reason the random-directed person needs only to identify with a peer-group. He does not, however, allow it to dominate him. If his sense of personhood is ruffled he will not hesitate to show a fury of which the neo-tribalist is incapable. Fortunately, he does not have the pushiness of the other-directed person. Because he is not involved in the personhood of another, he can be as detached as any individualist. He has forsaken the neo-tribal aggressiveness, and is at home among the flower children, with their "peace and joy" slogans. Unlike the neo-tribalist, he is able and willing to be an un-person. His world is strung across a backdrop of chaos and despair. For him the past and future are so blended into the present that time is almost without form or meaning. Hence it is not only possible, but necessary, to live dangerously. Since life is seen as a Theatre of the Absurd, only singular acts can provide the garment of personhood; persuasion no longer counts. Personifying acts do not have to be "constructive." It is creative to destroy the dead past. It is fulfilling to overthrow outworn institutions. This, in fact, is the political platform of random-directed man.

The philosophy of random-direction is existential. Life and belief must be limited to what can be experienced and felt. Observable nature provides the only forms for behavior, and it sets the limits of choice. The best course is that of feeling—without the restriction of caution or conscience.

The language of random-direction has no limits set upon it. However, there is one word that is always profane—the word *ought*. Man's wants are the only ought, and the good is within his grasp. Life is not a timid spark, as with the neo-tribal conformist. It is a flame of radical decision—of responsibility earned and borne. The random-directed man seeks to live bravely and creatively. He is willing to run the risk of alienation. He is willing to become a nonentity if, by so doing, he can find meaning and authenticity. *Authenticity* is, in fact, the hallmark of his identity. This is a radically different trait than *acceptance*, which is the hallmark of other-direction.

The random-directed person is a man-by-intention. He is as nearly as possible a self-made man. He finds a pattern that is right for him, and he tailors it to himself. This means that life is viewed as a drama instead of a historical process. Personhood is a role. It is only, however, in playing one's role that one acquires a *persona*. The role must be played with sincerity and conviction. This is made especially necessary by the doctrine of behaviorism. The individual overcomes its limitation by *making* that role come true. He has not only to fight the social scientists' dictum. He has to fight the neo-tribalists' interpretation that limits freedom to the group. He insists upon something the individualist never believed—that no two entities can possibly be alike. Here is what random-direction rejects in the older individualism: its myth that all men are made in the image of One. This myth contradicts the theology of neo-individualism. It is not only pointless, therefore, to follow examples, but also wrong.

Irreality of Random-Direction

The new forms of tribalism and individualism have only a superficial resemblance to the patterns they unconsciously ape. Something is lost in their rejection of these patterns. It includes an objectivity that can only be held by those who accept the otherness of the *given*. It also includes the virtues of faith and obedience, found in those who attend on an Other. Because of this basic defect, the virtues that collectivists strive for are obtained at the cost of real humanity. In recent decades we have seen how fascists and communists by the millions have exchanged humanity for solidarity. We have now seen random-directed persons make another kind of exchange. By the late sixties, freedom and privacy had become so precious that seemingly they could be had only by denying all debt to society. Collegians felt that their identity required an end to college authority and military conscription. This was a radical shift from the old and real individualism. The youngsters' inner-directed forebears had been secure enough to admit the need for authority and for keeping the peace. They accepted the draft as a patriotic duty. Compulsory class attendance seemed to them as reasonable as compulsory breathing. The only obligation they grumbled about was compulsory attendance at chapel.

In the process that leads to random-direction a curious myopia develops. People lose the ability to discern the real in form and function and meaning. Even faced with order in nature, they deny what to other people are the simple facts of life. Further, they cannot see that custom is society's safeguard against inexperience and lack of wisdom. They do not have Chesterton's insight into tradition as a democracy of the living *and* the dead—giving a voice to all who have ever found meaning in life.[3] They do not appreciate that much of reality can be expressed only in terms of symbol and myth. They suffer, without even knowing it, from a mental and moral handicap. They cannot accept as factors any knowledge or truth that they have not yet taken into account. Faced with this reality, their stock response is, "You cannot give answers to questions we will not ask."

Rapidity of Transition

One of the peculiarities of today's collectivism is that it has polarized far more rapidly than it did in ancient times. In Rome the period of other-direction lasted for a number of centuries. The transition from other- to random-direction lasted for several centuries more. By contrast, in the modern West other-direction has lasted for only a few decades—a century at the most. The period of transition to random-direction promises to be equally short. While the comparison of the two cultures belongs to the coming chapter, we must touch upon it here. To know the reasons for the change, and for the speedup in transition, is to know something about random-direction itself.

There is a close relation between social personality and political systems and events. There is also a relation between the forms of personhood and the forms of communication. Both in Rome and in the contemporary world random-direction came on the heels of political failure. It was marked by a failure in individual responsibility, to be sure; but it also attended the failure of a power system. In each case that power system was a type of imperialism— one that had grown, in fact, from a national to an international imperialism. In each case random-direction was expressed in disillusion and frustration—as an alienation of the soul. Men lacked the vitality to meet their commitments. They felt they were overextended. A shift from other- to random-direction helped them rationalize cutting back their commitments.

In Rome, as the Empire lost its early vitality, the demands for coordination and defense were more than the homeland could bear. Mercenaries had to be hired from among the conquered to protect the Empire from other, more fearsome barbarians. Eventually they had to protect Rome itself, after the mercenaries had taken the reins of power and set themselves upon the throne. The Empire failed because its citizens could not handle the demands put upon them for personal and social responsibility. They then turned their backs on the whole idea of neo-tribal involvement, and adopted the stance of disinvolvement.

This is happening in our own time as well. Random-direction is both a response to and a cause of the failure of neo-tribalism. While the youngsters of the 1960s were theoretically for involvement, they resisted the collective security of the free world, which was a form of neo-tribalism. They were isolationist both in their politics and in their sense of personhood. Their protest against the cold war—and especially against its "hotting up" in Viet Nam— was their way of moralizing against neo-tribalism.

Speedup in Communications

There is another factor that explains the speedup in transition. In ancient Rome the transition from other- to random-direction was slowed by a decay in communications. As the power of the Empire declined, news began to travel more slowly. The slowdown continued even though the boundaries were contracted and the frontiers shortened. There was no longer the facility or even the will to communicate. The legions were withdrawn, and trade and travel ceased. The roads became overgrown for lack for use. Detachment was inevitable. Men were regressing into what eventually became a feudal tribalism.

By contrast, our own transition to random-direction has been intensified by a speedup in communication. If Marshall McLuhan is right, the changes in communications media have contributed greatly to random-direction. In his book, *Understanding Media: The Extensions of Man*, McLuhan has given us clues to understanding some of the differences in social personality. He has also given clues to the causes of transition. McLuhan associates the visual medium of print with individualism and detachment. He associates the aural medium of radio with other-direction—that is, with neo-tribalism. He has demonstrated the effect of the "mosaic" or "tactual" medium of television upon the newest generation. Print and television are "cool," and permit detachment. Both contribute to individualism. They differ considerably, however, in their effect upon identity. Print requires the whole to be seen by summing up its parts. Television only allows things to be seen in relation. The parts can never be taken out of context. Print looks at the trees, while television looks at the forest. Therefore television, while encouraging detachment by its coolness, requires involvement by the way the message is given. Radio, by contrast, is "high definition," and *only* allows involvement. It has a far more powerful effect than the other media upon the emotions. McLuhan believes that radio and public address systems (also "hot") were causes of the wave of neo-tribalism that engulfed Germany in the 1930s. He asserts that had television existed the war might not have taken place. On the "low-definition" medium of TV Hitler would have shown up as a comic—and not as a charismatic—character.

McLuhan makes a good case in showing how the electronic media have had the effect of retribalizing man. He has also shown—although without specifically saying so—how it can reindividualize man. His thesis explains, to a degree, the difference between the old individualism and the new. The youngster who is molded by television is very different from the earlier individualist, who was molded by print. He possesses a world-view that is integral rather than fragmental, amateur and inclusive rather than analytical and professional. His comprehension of life is holistic rather than compartmentalized.

The effect of media upon random-direction is far from singular, however. The transistor radio has the opposite effect from that of television. It will not allow the individual's detachment, even when by himself. It takes the youngster by the ear, and destroys all chance for silence. There is another medium that is more involving still. It is the electronic amplification system, put to the service of rock music. What the transistor does for the individual, rock does for the group. Here are the "hottest" of all media and of all messages. Together they have the greatest effect in retribalizing the group. Rather than bringing the youngsters into conformity with their elders, however, it merely consolidates random-direction.

Creative Possibilities in Random-Direction

This, of course, shows the possibility of destruction of identity for random-directed people. What, however, of the *normal* character of random-direction? What is the possibility for the youngster who is able to keep his cool, and to build a social identity? With experience and judgment, he might hope to adjust to life as well as his inner-directed forebear. He is far less likely than his other-directed parents to panic. He maintains his cool while others fret about his inability to speed-read, his unwillingness to plan ahead, and his inability to regard work as an end in itself. In spite of his depth-involvement, he is better able than his parents to take risks and make decisions. His weaknesses are revealed chiefly by contrast with inner-direction. Lacking the conviction of the old individualist—and the driving force of the puritan ethic—he is unable to fulfil his role with any real vitality. His depth-involvement becomes a handicap in the field of action, where detachment is an asset. He overidentifies with those he is involved with, and so is deprived of the ability to be practical. Being anti-tradition, he is anti-institution. He cannot distinguish between the institutions that give life and those that destroy it. Being of this mind, he dare not think of persons as anything but *ends*, and therefore he cannot put them to institutional use. He cannot in any case be a real executive, because he has an impoverished sense of structure and function. He understands only shared leadership, which is government by committee. Therefore he is a lamb among wolves when it comes to the uses of power. He can generate plenty of power, but he cannot control or govern it.*

The most characteristic trait of random-direction is its rejection of authority and order. It cannot believe there may be rules that apply to all mankind. Each must be allowed to find his own. The random-directed man cannot think of himself as subordinate to a society, so he resists all shaping and molding. By contrast, the earlier individual

* This raises the question as to which social type is most effective with institutions. Because of his sense of involvement and his hyperactivity, it might seem to be the neo-tribalist. Despite this, I believe it is the inner-directed man who is best at dealing with institutions. He is not so anxious about the future as the neo-tribalist, and he is better in touch with the past. He has a sense of history, purpose, and function. He is able by himself to decide and to act. He can mobilize the present into a well-defined future, using his own skills and the experience of the past. His combination of detachment and sympathy give him the best combination for co-ordinating persons and events.

was molded at length. He was shaped first by parental discipline, and later by the abrasive and polishing action of external events and involvements. He became through process, and not by simply willing it. Self-denial and privation had a positive value for him. So did suffering and sorrow. These were the crucible in which precious mettle was refined.

Ambivalence in Identifying

An ambivalence may be noted here in what has been said about random-directed people. There is a discrepancy between the involvement they profess and the disinvolvement that is so apparent to others. This ambivalence is real. It belongs to random-direction. With John Donne, random-direction professes involvement with all mankind. Yet it has one enormous area of disinvolvement. It accepts the "other," but it totally rejects its own. Because it is in protest against the neo-tribalism from which it sprang, it must disclaim *its* entanglements. It rejects the institutions, the security pacts, the morals and the identity of the neo-tribalist. Its capacity to be totally involved, therefore, is quite limited. It identifies empathetically with the "not one's own." It disidentifies antipathetically with the "one's own." This is the most radical kind of identification. It identifies in a way that is contrary to nature itself. It leads its proponents into the pathetic fallacy. They identify with those who are utterly other—whose intention may well be to destroy them.

An ambiguity persists in other-direction as well. It suggests, in fact, where the new form got its weakness. While the random-directed man cannot help overidentifying with the "other," the other-directed person is likely to do this too. He will not necessarily do so, since neo-tribalism has taught him to be against the "other." But he cannot be trusted on his own. He has no given basis for judgment, and is forced to make a personal response. Therefore his society must protect him against exposure to the "other." This is why neo-tribalism must keep its citizens in a straitjacket. It can be sure of them only by using propaganda, rallies, group-think, synthetic symbols, and a forced mystique. It has to discourage any identifying between the "one's own" and the "not one's own." There is great loss of face when the neo-tribalist defects. Yet, if exposed as an individual to the "other," this is what he is likely to do.

No such ambivalence exists for the traditional types of personhood. Both tribalists and individualists can distinguish between the "one's own" and the "not one's own." What is more, they can keep the distinction in mind, no matter how involved. It is only among collectivists that there is an internalized pressure not to make a distinction. Their ambivalence is shown in the following chart:

Emotional Response and Impulse-to-Identify in Four Types of Social Personality

Identity types	*Response to and identification with:*	
	"One's own"	*"Not one's own"*
Tribal	Empathy	Apathy
Individual	Sympathy	Sympathy
Neo-tribal	Empathy	Antipathy
Neo-individual	Antipathy	Empathy

A Variant of Collectivism

We may ask, "Is neo-individualism really a form of collective personality? If so, is it not a contradiction to call it individual?" The answer is that random-direction is individual in *intention*, but collective in *fact*. The proof of its *individual intention* lies in the political activity of random-directed people. They are against every form of neo-tribalism—whether it be communism, fascism, or the makeshift alliances of the free nations. As neo-isolationists, they repudiate the contracts for collective security that neo-tribalists feel bound to honor.

The proof of their *collectivism* lies in their concept of justice. There is no sense of individual morality or of individual justice in random-direction. The private ethic that dealt with sex, work, and property has been replaced

by a new set of absolutes—the ethic of collective morality—dealing with war, welfare, and civil rights. The new
absolutes are quite as total in their way as the old absolutes once had been. For the random-directed, this ethic is
a matter of the deepest obligation. It is equally binding
upon all persons, regardless of their sense of identity.

It is, in fact, upon the authority of this ethic that
random-direction has based its hostility to other-direction.
Until the random-directed protest began, the neo-tribalists
had been collective in symbols and identity, without ever
having gotten around to installing the new morality. This
to the random-directed appeared to be the worst kind of
hypocrisy.

And here is the reason for the recent change in people's
values and behavior. By and large, other-direction has
capitulated to the random-directed rebellion. It has quailed
before its fierceness and been ashamed in the face of its
logic. Because it is concerned with acceptance by persons,
rather than with intrinsic value and order, it has let the
random-directed have their way. It has admitted the inconsistency of having a collective identity and an individual
morality. In so doing, it has quite uncritically accepted the
concept of group guilt.

The difficulty with other-direction, in its own postwar
transition, was that it was never quite collective. It had a
residue of the puritan ethic and only an embryonic sense
of group morality. Random-direction, despite its individualist intent, is the first *true* form of collectivism to arrive
upon the scene. It is the first form of social identity to
make a deliberate break with tradition. It is the first to
regard history as irrelevant. It is the first since the genuinely tribal to accept group guilt as an indisputable reality.
Jeremiah, Ezekiel and age-long experience notwithstand-
ing, it *forces* the son to bear the father's sins.

Random-Direction's New Morality

Despite the conviction of random-directed people,
group guilt is basically immoral. It is the same concept, in
fact, that communists have used in brainwashing their

victims, and have chosen to use for themselves. This is because they are totally neo-tribal, and because group guilt is the only punishment that can wipe out private identity. Edward Hunter has commented upon this in *Brainwashing*, the book he wrote as a result of the Korean experience:

> In (the communist) framework, individual guilt is a minor matter; what weighs heaviest upon a man is his guilt as a member of a collectivity. He is guilty for the sins of his forebears, and for all of the wrongs committed by his kind. The limitless-responsibility theory has him hemmed in. He loses a sense of individuality in time or space. Confession becomes easier that way, and voluntarily, of crimes he never committed, of crimes that never took place. Whether they actually happened, in the form confessed, becomes irrelevant. What is relevant is his need to cleanse himself of this heavy burden.[4]

The degree to which Americans have accepted the doctrine of group guilt is shown in the way many churches responded to the Black Manifesto in the summer of 1969. The reparations demanded by James Forman and his followers arose from a very different sense of justice than that expressed in the Law of Moses. Moses said only that the children must *suffer* for the sins of the fathers. Collectivist justice demands far more. It requires that the children must *atone* for the sins of the fathers. This is the "theology" of reparations.

The Question of Conscience Formation

As we look back it is easy enough to see how the West came to adopt the symbols and concepts of collective identity. It is not easy, however, to understand why we have suddenly been consumed by a sense of group guilt. If it is true that conscience is *taught*, the problem is only compounded. How did random-direction acquire such strong convictions about collective justice? Why is it so steeped in group guilt? In seeking an answer to this we are not helped by Marshall McLuhan, who is more ready to ascribe it to magic than to any rational process:

> The new feeling that people have about guilt is not something that can be privately assigned to some individual, but is, rather, something shared by everybody, in some mysterious way.... This feeling is an aspect of the new mass culture we are moving into—a world of total involvement in which everybody is so profoundly involved with everybody else and in which nobody can really imagine what private guilt can be anymore.[5]

Actually, the process is quite rational. The only element of mystery is that it happened without our knowing it. In retrospect we can understand it. The trainers of random-direction have been people who shared the responsibility for bringing the youngsters up, and who had what the parents did not have—convictions. They were men and women who had already been collectivized. Most were professional people—teachers, clergy, psychologists, counsellors, social workers, and the like. These people valued responsibility, but had already broken with tradition. All they needed to do was to be themselves—to voice their beliefs and to show their commitment. In so doing, they transferred their values and their sense of identity to the youngsters whom they were subconsciously training.*

There is one element in the collectivist conscience that the trainers did not put there, however. It is the *negative* element, without which there can be no real conscience. This element is present in random-direction in a quite remarkable way. But it was not instilled in the youngsters by the trainers I have mentioned. They have never said to their charges, "Thou shalt not." They have been permissive rather than strict, accepting rather than critical. Where, then, did the negative training come from? My guess is that it has come largely from the propaganda of the communist

---

*It is inevitable that the younger generation—or at least the bourgeois segment of it that is now random-directed—should absolutize its values. Only in the stage of transition do men have such a psychic weakness that they are guided by persons rather than by principles. Other-direction has been that stage of transition. It is likely that once other-directed people have accepted collectivist morality, collectivism will be whole and complete. Neo-tribalism and neo-individualism will then be only variants within a universal type, for whom the only political entity will be the world.

nations. For many years our news media have been loaded
with vituperation. This has been a constant throughout the
youngsters' childhood. Few people have tried to explain it
to them, for they supposed that the young people were
immune to it even as their elders were. But they were not
immune. Their parents were able to see the propaganda for
what it was, because their personalities were already
formed. But the young people could not regard the propaganda in any historical perspective. They took it personally. They were unable to be disinvolved from the
blame that was heaped upon them and upon their kindred.
The communists failed to convert them to their form of
neo-tribalism, but they imparted all too well their understanding of justice. The young people made it their dogma.
What is more, the youngsters now were able to do what
the communists had always failed at: they shamed and
embarrassed their elders into accepting the tenets of collective morality and justice.

Some Underlying Doctrines

The primary basis of random-direction, as of all collectivism, is the doctrine of behaviorism. There are other
foundation-stones, however. One is the *subjective idealism*
that was a variant on the thought of Socrates and Plato. It
saw reality not in the object, but in its interpretation by
the subject. Another basis is the fourteenth-century teaching of *nominalism* that was propounded by William of
Ockham. William paved the way for the collectivist's dismissal of structure and function. He claimed there was no
objective reality in the distinctions we make between
things—distinctions that are expressed in the nomenclature
we give them. The cutting edge of the axiom that is known
as *Occam's Razor* is this: "Entities must not be unnecessarily multiplied." William of Ockham gave the existentialist
an excuse for being blind to the pattern of another in
himself.

The random-directed view of man is one of autonomy.
This is the intrinsic pattern it claims to see: every man is
free from the claim of every "other." He is free to relate to

God or man if he wishes; but he is equally free not to do so. He can get along by himself. The historical view of this autonomy was expressed by Leo Tolstoy:

> If every man were free, that is, if every man could act as he chose, the whole of history would be a tissue of disconnected accidents.[6]

The theological view of this autonomy is expressed by William Hamilton, one of the radical theologians:

> There is no God-shaped blank within man. . . . God is not in the realm of the necessary at all. . . . He is one of the possibilities in a radically pluralistic spiritual and intellectual universe.[7]

In its view of man, random-direction sees a pattern of multiple autonomies, just as inner-direction had done. Each man, in order to be a person, must have the capacity of being an island unto himself. The two types differ radically, however, in their orientation to God. Inner-direction never sought an autonomy that would set it free from God. Random-direction, by contrast, insists upon such an autonomy. The old individualism was only inner-directed so far as *men* were concerned. Random-direction is inner-directed only so far as *God* is concerned. Its true community is with man. This is why it is collectivistic, and why it cannot under any circumstances be genuinely individualistic. It must always be involved with man. Its declaration of independence sets it free only from absolutes. It does this by having a philosophy of poly-autonomy.

The true religion of random-direction is polytheism. We can find an illustration of this in a remark of William Blake, the poet-artist admired by many in the counterculture. Blake was a mystic who identified deeply with the sensory world, but not with principles of order. He was devoted to Jesus, but had only contempt for the Father and Lawgiver. Blake's point of view is recorded by his friend Crabb Robinson,

> On our *tete a tete* walk home at night (I) put the popular question to him, concerning the imputed Divinity of Jesus

Christ. He answered: "He is the only God."—but then he added—"And so am I and so are you."[8]

Random-direction's essential humanism is revealed in one of Blake's epigrams, "Thou art a man, God is no more,/ Thine own humanity learn to adore." Its naturalism is illustrated in another, "Sooner murder an infant in its cradle than nurse unacted desires." Its disinvolvement from God is shown in a third, " 'Come hither, my boy, and tell what thou seest there,'/ 'A fool tangled in a religious snare.' " Its anti-institutional bent is evident in Blake's motto, "I must Create a System or be enslav'd by another Man's,/ I will not Reason & Compare: my business is to Create." Its inability to see a common pattern for mankind is shown in another of Blake's proverbs, "One Law for the Lion and Ox is Oppression."[9]

The shortcomings of the random-directed mind must ever keep its dreams from coming true. Isaiah's vision—of the day when the lion will eat straw like the ox—springs from a radically different set of preconceptions. It looks for a peace that is wrought by God himself—a perfect union of justice, love, and power. Compared with this grand design, no worth can be found in a union of power with random-direction's twin deities—autonomy and anarchy.

Notes on Chapter Four:

1. David Riesman (with Nathan Glazer and Reuel Denney), *The Lonely Crowd* (New Haven: Yale University Press, 1965), p. 110.
2. John Dewey, *Human Nature and Conduct* (New York: Henry Holt, 1922), p. 6.
3. G. K. Chesterton, *Orthodoxy* (Garden City, N.Y.: Doubleday, 1959), p. 48.
4. Edward Hunter, *Brainwashing* (New York: Farrar, Straus and Cudahy, 1962), p. 236.
5. Marshall McLuhan, *The Medium is the Massage* (New York: Bantam Books, 1967), p. 61.
6. Leo Tolstoy, *War and Peace*, Epilogue, Part II, Chapter 8.
7. Thomas J. J. Altizer and William Hamilton, *Radical Theology and the Death of God* (New York: Bobbs-Merrill, 1966), p. 40.
8. Alfred Kazin, editor, *The Pocket Blake* (New York: Viking Press, 1967), p. 680.
9. *Ibid.*, pp. 11, 255, 135, 460, 264.

TYPES OF
SOCIAL IDENTITY:

A SUMMARY

Corporate Personality

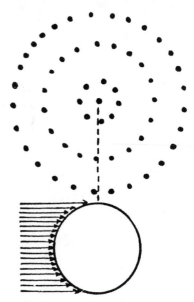

The circle represents the individual. The arrows represent authority, which in this case comes from the past. The individual has private obligations but he has no personal rights. He sees himself only as a member of an organism. His cosmos is a series of concentric circles—family, village, and tribe. Tribal personality is marked by differentiation in its members. There is no homogenizing of persons or values. Members are distinguished by age, sex, size, skill, social status, and charismatic gifts. The governing sanction is *shame*. This brings the individual, after a deviation, into conformity with the group through contrition, confession, absolution, and restoration. Deviation is quickly detected because the entire organism is hurt by one member's offense. The group is corporately responsible for an injury to a member of another group. When a fault has been committed, guilt settles upon the corporate person, and shame is felt by all. The locus, however, is in the offending member. The individual cannot break with the group. His only identification is with the body. Outside the body he is an un-person. Hence shame is a sufficient sanction: it forces the member to act in his own behalf.

Advantages:
Accepts self with own limitations
Has convictions
Functions well in normal environment

Disadvantages:
Does not easily adjust to outsiders
Does not carry sense of autonomy or responsibility outside the
    group
Intense preoccupation with *face.*

Individual Personality

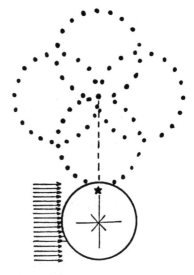

The circles represent the multiple associations of the individualist. He is at the center because he is the only member whom all of the groups have in common. He is not totally involved with any group. Therefore he is partially detached from them all. He is no longer *only* a member; now he is a *person*. The external force of authority has finally been reduced. Detachment has made it necessary for authority to be *internalized* as well. Internal direction is suggested by the compass rose. This does not give the individual autonomy in respect to *authority*—only in respect to *persons*. His response to authority is still response to an Other. In being value- rather than person-oriented, he can make a dependable internal response. As with the tribalist, functional differentiation is essential. At this stage it may be seen in the differentiation of *groups*. The individualist is not, like the tribalist, highly concerned with "face." He can be himself wherever he goes. To him shame is only a childhood sanction. His grownup sanction is *guilt*. Guilt is not relieved by companying with others; it is absolved by God alone. Therefore the individual's true corporality is with God. This gives him the capacity to have a basic detachment in the midst of multiple involvements. This detachment is the source of his vitality and power.

Advantages:
Has clear sense of own personhood
Has convictions and the moral courage to express them
Is resourceful, willing to take on responsibility
Is mobile, can maintain selfhood anywhere

Disadvantages:
Insensitive to others' feelings
Has difficulty in expressing own feelings
Likely to be task-oriented
Has difficulty in voiding guilt feelings

Other-direction

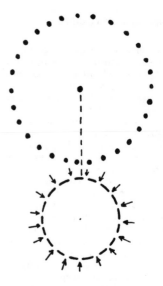

Multiple associations exist for the other-directed individual, but the one having priority is the one-making-demands-right-now. For this reason the neo-tribalist's associations are shown as a single group. Whether they are related or not, he sees them as a neo-tribal unity. The values and membership of each is changing, however; there simply is no constant. Therefore the individual must ever be on the alert to sense the whims and moods of his groups. Hence the need for *anxiety*. Anxiety cannot be alleviated, however, as guilt and shame may be. It is the constant in collectivism—a symptom of collective identity. Here the individual must be homogeneous with every other; differences are "undemocratic." This gives a picture of the self as a smooth but broken circle, representing the traits of openness, tolerance, and interchangeability. Individuality is forbidden to come to light, and corporality cannot emerge; the ever changing life and standards reflect the group's want of identity and power. The upshot is collective personality—a poor alternative to the first two. The emptiness of collectivism is reflected in its uncertainty both in being and believing.

Advantages:
Sensitive to others' wants and needs
Is process-oriented
Adjusts well to others

Disadvantages:
Has indefinite sense of own personhood because always under pressure to change personality on demand
Is unable to express strong convictions
Is ill at ease in own company
Has difficulty voiding anxiety

Random-direction

An attempt to be inner-directed, random-direction is the reaction against the pull of the group by the basically other-directed. It recognizes only informal groups. The claims of family, church, nation, and culture are all disavowed. Other-direction's values are retained: functionlessness, tolerance, and sincerity. Relationships are comparable to casual, one-to-one, kinetic collisions of identical molecules. Individual sense of being is whole but irregular, since effected by collision rather than by the abrasive processes of tradition, function, and negative sanction. No claims of the past or future are recognized—only those of

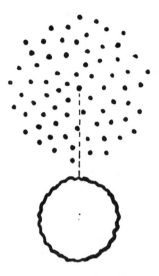

the existential *now*. Freed from residual puritanism, the need is for uninhibited self-expression showing creativity and power. Personality is not achieved deterministically by associations, but by the individual's intention. Intention-to-be-a-person mirrors the need to end the other-directed sense of anxiety and the new sense of alienation. It reflects the desire to fill a useful, self-chosen role. "Face" is still a factor of enormous importance. The mood is a reaction against the aggressiveness and impersonality of the members of an other-directed society. It is more of a mood, however, than genuine personhood. Being *for involvement*, it keeps its head in the sand.

Advantages:
Can assert independence from the pull of the group
Is sensitive to the needs of others, yet maintains self-reliance
Avoids chameleonism of other-direction by honesty in one-to-one relationships

Disadvantages:
Lacks sense of tradition and an overriding purpose in life
Has poorly developed sense of corporality, cannot avoid sense of alienation
Cannot achieve responsible freedom for want of transcendent symbols
Unable to accept universal values
Follows feelings rather than reason
Tends to become neurotically consumed with group guilt

Chapter Five

A CYCLE
OF SOCIAL IDENTITY

There have been, in man's history, two lengthy eras of individualism. Each belonged to the West, and each was the crown of its culture. The first age was that of the ancient Greco-Roman world. The second was that of the modern West. The earlier age began in the ninth century before Christ, and ended in the first. The second began in the twelfth century of our era, and ended in the early decades of the twentieth century. Each epoch had a duration of about eight hundred years.

While these were the only ages in which many people developed a sense of individuality, the trait has not been denied to those of other times or places. Men and women have been able to develop individuality wherever they have had unrelated associations that were bound by a common set of values and symbols. The possibility has been relatively limited, however, for people of continental cultures. It has been more available to seafarers, for whom personal mobility has been a real achievement.

There was no widespread individualism in any of the cultures that preceded the Greek. In each, personal mobility was restricted to a relatively small number of persons. I refer to the cultures of Egypt, Mesopotamia, Syria, and Iran—all of which flowered earlier than the Greek—and to those of India and China, which were contemporary with the Greek. Each of these was a continental culture. Its leaders were the only members who could develop either

94

mobility or multiplicity in their relationships; other members of these societies remained static. As a consequence each of these cultures moved from tribalism to tribal confederacy to a kind of national collectivism. The chiefs became super-chiefs, and finally kings and emperors. The result—the Oriental potentate—is the pattern for the dictator of today. In such cultures as these, people never developed any independence. They could think of themselves only as totally involved.

Individualism in the Ancient World

The first people who became individualists were the Greeks. Roman and Hebrew individualism lagged the Greek by some two centuries because the Greeks had readier access to the sea, and because they were forced to venture abroad. Early in their history the Greeks' land had been deforested. The resultant soil erosion required them to find food elsewhere. Fortunately, their maritime location made it unnecessary for them to migrate. They met their needs by becoming a nation of seafarers and traders.

There was another factor that promoted individualism among the Greeks. The land itself turned people's eyes to the sea. Its rugged mountains made travel by foot very difficult, which not only secured the Greeks from foreign invasion, but made them relatively safe from one another as well. For this reason their society became subdivided into numerous *poleis*, or *city-states*. The *polis* was a larger entity than a tribe, yet it was small enough for its citizens to know one another. It never became so large that its members' identity had to be abstracted from a corporate to a collective sense of personhood. The earliest rulers of the *poleis* were kings. Later, as a sense of individualism began to prevail, the city-states were governed by oligarchies of aristocrats, and still later by the people themselves.

Democracy came early to Greece. It both sprang from and encouraged a widespread sense of individuality. While Greek democracy did not allow citizenship to everyone, it conferred it upon most. Moreover, townsmen and countrymen were treated alike; the franchise gave equality as well as liberty. The small size of their communities gave the possibility for absolute, rather than representative, democracy. Every citizen participated in drawing up the laws by which he was governed.

Greek individualism was thus like that of the early Americans. The New England founders were also settled in communities that were inaccessible by land. Yet they were open to one another by a sea that washed upon many safe and accessible harbors. The New England communities were separate, but they were not far apart.

The Greeks' extension of associations began in the eleventh century. They established trading posts in Egypt and Asia Minor, in the Aegean Sea, and in the Mediterranean as far as Sicily and Italy. This enterprise was begun by individual city-states, but it soon became cooperative. Its participants thereupon became responsibly involved not only with men of other Greek communities, but with those of other nations as well. They worked, for example, with the Phoenicians, whose trading activities had been longer established and more far-ranging than their own.

Personal mobility does not, in itself, make individuality possible. Were this the case, the Vikings would have been more individualistic than the Greeks. The Vikings' enterprise was not one, however, that encouraged multiple relationships. The Vikings were buccaneers, not traders. Like the Chinese pirates who bottled up Japan for so many centuries, they were clansmen. The Vikings' forays took them across the Atlantic and throughout the Mediterranean. Their river boats made them masters of much of the continent. They had a free hand in the Danube and the Volga, and they ranged as far as Constantinople. Yet they were tribesmen from beginning to end. They never entered into responsible, unrelated associations with other peoples.

In some respects the Phoenicians were like the Vikings. They were the most bold and adventurous seafarers of the earlier age. Because they were traders, however, they entered into responsible and unrelated associations. Many of them, therefore, became individualists. But like the Jews— who were also traders—their basic identity was corporate.

They did not have an island mentality. They were continentals. They could not be detached, as were the Greeks in their peninsular fastness.

The Greeks, by contrast with the Jews and Phoenicians, became pure individualists. Although in the course of time they moved from inner- to random-direction, they never acquired the mentality of other-directedness. This was partly because they never really became a nation, and partly because, having no population explosion, they never needed a puritan ethic. Except in wartime, they never pressed the individual into the service of the state.

Nearly all the city-states were individualist by the criteria we have considered. Athens became the greatest because of its accessibility: it was easily reached by land as well as by sea. Consequently its citizens adopted an attitude of openness to other peoples—one that was especially appropriate because of the Athenians' own energetic independence. The Athenians were men of the world. Their wealth and leisure made possible the highest refinement of art, science, and philosophy.

The Spartans were quite different from the Athenians, and in fact from the rest of Greece. Sparta was the most remote of the city-states; its contacts with the outside world were the fewest. Its citizens did not show the ambition, inventiveness, and curiosity that were found elsewhere in Greece. They devoted themselves to the arts of war, and to masculine hardness and discipline. Consequently, when their inner-direction began to fail, they did not move on to random-direction. They sought to recover their corporality, and got collectivism instead.

In seeking to recover their tribal unity, the Spartans were hindered by one thing. Their economy was based upon slavery. Their slaves were the Helots—descendants of the aboriginal Greeks. To keep a large minority in check, the Spartans recruited a secret police. Both the slaves within and ideologies without gave the Spartans an enemy. Here was the reason for their puritan ethic: they were bottled up in their own land. Because of this, they developed a planned economy that further restricted their freedom. Their collectivism was the more aggressive because of the individuality they had known. Even sex was pressed into the service of the Spartan state. When women were married to less than the fittest, they were required to bear children to warriors.

Individualism in the Modern World

Before going on to the proofs of individualism, let us see how it arose in the modern world. The process is nearly parallel with that of ancient times. When the Dark Ages had run their course, the Germanic invaders had become Christians, and were settled *in situ*. They were no longer nomadic hunters, but herdsmen and agriculturalists. They had adapted their tribalism to the system they had over-run. With the dying Empire thus reborn as the Holy Roman Empire, men reverted from collectivism into cor-porality.

Feudal society differed from tribal only in replacing the circle with a pyramid. At the bottom were the serfs and the villains. Above were the nobles and lords. At the top were the Emperor and the Pope. The temporal order was immutable. Only in the ranks of the clergy could a man move from one level to another, and this partly because of his sacral function and partly because, having neither family nor property, his mobility posed no threat to the status quo. As a result, the whole society could accept the unifying bond of values and symbols that religion gave.

Let us try to pinpoint the emergence of individualism from the feudal system. Because the historical evidence is not as accessible as the biblical record, we must deduce the time and the place. The time can only be that of the Crusades. It is in this period that we see the dissolution of feudalism, the development of towns, and the rise of scholasticism. The place must be Paris, and for several reasons: (a) northern Europe was more uniformly tribal than the south, (b) the French people were the major participants in the Crusades, and (c) Paris was the one great city of the French. We find, early in the twelfth century, two proofs of what we are looking for. One is the earliest university, whose master, Peter Abelard, began to teach about 1115. Another is the Gothic architecture that originated in Paris simultaneously with the university. Until 1120—twenty years after the First Crusade—the French had an indifferent kind of architecture. Given the pointed arch, which the crusaders had discovered in Syria, and the need for a new expression of identity, the Parisian school produced the art form that was to be linked with nationalism and individualism for the next four hundred years. The first Gothic building was the Abbey Church of St. Denis, completed in 1144 as a shrine to the Apostle of France. It became the immediate focal point, not only of French spirituality but of patriotism as well. It marked the alliance of the kings of France with the bishops of their realm, and with the cities under those bishops' authority. It was probably the first expression in the modern West of national and individual identity.

Links Between Individualism and Nationalism

Such an argument is, of course, open to question. The rise of nationalism is not necessarily accompanied by a sense of individual identity. Some peoples, like the Greeks, became individualistic because they did *not* develop the usual kind of nationalism. Yet the biblical record—which is not only the most accessible, but the clearest—shows individualism to be very closely linked with Old Testament nationalism.

Fortunately, for a gentile world that left no clear record of its concepts of personhood, we have one that is as dependable, in its way, as the Bible itself. It is the artistic output of the periods of rising individualism. The two great ages of individualism coincided with the two great ages of art. The Golden Age and the Renaissance expressed the joy of man at being released from the tribal prison into a genuine individuality. The beginnings of these periods mark the transition to individualism, and the fullest flowerings of these periods mark the fullest flowering of individualism.

Of the two eras, the more interesting one for social identity is the earlier one. The Renaissance came about, to a large degree, through the West's rediscovery of what earlier man had been and done. Crusading Westerners met Saracens who had their own sense of individuality, and who had held it through the Dark Ages, when Westerners had lost their own. They brought back the cultural treasures the Muslims had guarded, and which the Church had allowed to slip out of its hands. These were the treasures of Greek science and learning. Thus the Renaissance men had access, at the beginning of their individualism, to the lore of the past. The earlier peoples had had to start from scratch.

Individualism Among Greeks, Romans, and Jews

There is another reason for our interest in the earlier age. It is the remarkable effect that release from tribalism had on three very different peoples—the Greeks, the Romans, and the Jews. With the Greeks the Golden Age meant a concern with truth and beauty in its purest sense. It meant mental speculation, and art to look at rather than to use. The Romans took their release quite differently. They were practical men of affairs—engineers, lawmakers, administrators, soldiers. They were the first individualists to develop a military-industrial complex. The Jewish expression of individualism was the great outpouring of moral and spiritual insight that is known as the Prophetic Movement. This movement began at the same time, in the northern kingdom, as did individualism; it was in the ninth century, in the time of the prophet Elijah. In the southern kingdom the Prophetic Movement lasted until about 200 B.C.—the time when individualism was beginning to disappear from the Greco-Roman world.

Greek individualism dates from about the ninth century before Christ. N. G. L. Hammond tells us that in this century the princely classes were individualistic, but that the commoners continued to be fraternalistic, bound by obligations and restraints from which their rulers were already largely exempt.[1] The transition to inner-direction is shown in the Homeric sagas that date back to the middle of the ninth century. Homer's Iliad looks back to the

Grecian past, recalling the tribal glory of earlier times. The virtues it extols are the martial virtues of loyalty, fellowship, and devotion. The Odyssey, by contrast, exhibits the individualist's sense of adventure, as well as his curiosity and resourcefulness. The Iliad provided the prototype for personhood that the Spartans sought to recapture. Odysseus was the pattern for the Athenian of the classical age.*

Popular Expressions of Change in Identity

When there is a change in a people's social identity, it seems that their poets and artists are the first to be consciously aware of it. The change is only confirmed later by men whose minds are reflective and impersonal—philosophers and theologians, for example. Yet, in spite of the artists' sensitivity, it is the people as a whole who are the first to express changes in identity, and their expression is a quite unconscious one.

Both in ancient and in modern times it was the people who were first aware of their transition from tribalism to individualism. Likewise, it was the people who were aware of the identity crisis that was leading to collectivism. In both periods the emergence of the individual was expressed in joy and excitement, and in a flowering of art and learning. In both periods the individual's submergence back into the group was expressed in a century of aimless and senseless wars. In each of these events the period of transition was signalled first in a change in the life style and outlook of whole peoples, and then by the successive expressions of artists, scholars, and theologians. The great classical art of Greece was produced after the Golden Age had ended. The exchange of art for philosophy—with a debasement both of art and religion—did not take place until the Greek wars of identity had already been fought. The Golden Age was not an age of individualism, but of transition to individualism. It was a time when men were

---

*It is not certain that Homer composed both the Iliad and the Odyssey. However, the two sagas are at most two or three generations apart.

still under the imprint of tribalism, but experiencing the joy and wonder of release. The ninth century was able to produce poets like Homer and Hesiod. Philosophers like Plato and Aristotle could not appear until the fourth century—long after the Golden Age had ended, and when inner-direction was beginning to be exchanged for random-direction. The classic artists had to come in an age when individualism was well developed, and when excellence could be based upon developed techniques. This was the fifth century, which produced men like Phidias, Sophocles, and Aristophanes.

The same is true of the Renaissance. The thirteenth century has often been described as the time of the greatest flowering of the human spirit. Yet its only popular art was that of men who worked in guilds, building the great cathedrals and churches that survive as a monument to that age. The individualist art of the Renaissance came long after the thirteenth century. Only a few individual artists, like Boccaccio and Chaucer, lived during the golden age that was the true rebirth. Those whose art was more individualistic and highly developed—like El Greco, Michelangelo, Leonardo, and Shakespeare—had to come later. Yet even *such* genius is limited by the time factor in a cycle of social identity. Genius reaches its limit when individualism is recognized as the norm. It is significant that, of the greatest Renaissance artists, only Shakespeare outlived Calvin and Luther. The Renaissance had to come to an end when the reformers put the stamp of divine approval upon individualism—and especially upon the puritan ethic. When the puritan ethic is introduced, artistic genius is not so likely to flourish.

Social Identity and the Puritan Ethic

Here we are faced with the need to consider the relation of the puritan ethic to individualism itself. The two do not necessarily go together, as has been seen in the case of Greece. A number of modern, individualist countries have gotten along without the puritan ethic. The Scandinavians have not required it, nor have the French or English.

Puritanism is chiefly needed in a land where the population is growing faster than the means of support, and where there is no place to export the surplus of people. The ethic leads men to set a premium upon labor as an end in itself, so that it can be regarded as a good. England never became puritan, even though it had a heavily puritan middle class. It had attractive colonies to which the puritans could be exported as fast as they were created. Germany, which was also puritan, could not do this. Its surplus of people were free to leave the country, but they could not remain under their country's aegis. Because Germany was a land power, and because it had no colonies to which its surplus could comfortably go, it resorted to military expansion.

The same was true of ancient Rome. By the time Roman trade and travel had gotten started, the Greeks and Phoenicians had established themselves throughout the Mediterranean. The Romans had to concentrate upon production and distribution at home, and in so doing they became puritan. They developed the power and the incentive to enlarge their borders; thus they followed a path that, in modern times, has been followed by Japan as well as Germany. It is now the path for Russia and China, and for the United States as well.*

---

*Because we have had no shortage of land, the United States has exported *capital*, rather than *people*. This has nonetheless created difficulties for the nations where this investment has gone.

Puritanism has continued to dominate the American scene and character. Our dedication to social welfare has committed us to a high consumption in order to justify a constant high volume of production. Yet it is an ethic that can be justified only when our needs are greater than our capacity to produce. Its blind continuance places a double yoke upon us all. We become slaves to the consumer-god in a setting where the customer is always right. We become slaves to the producer-god through our own internal demands for perfection. The net result is a drain in psychic power. While puritanism encourages good business, it exacts a high cost in personal and social tensions. A more realistic philosophy is that of the Oriental bazaar, "Let the buyer beware." Perhaps the best is that of the non-puritan British. No one who lived through the wartime experience can fail to appreciate a motto that sees both war and peace as games to be played and enjoyed, "Business as usual."

Puritanism inevitably gives a different interpretation to the meaning of individuality than does an individualism that is free from puritanism. The puritan is taught, early in childhood, to think of himself as being at the service of his society. He comes to think of himself as a means, not as an end. Where puritanism is still associated with inner-direction—still involved with religion, that is—the individual sees himself as a participant in a divine economy. Where puritanism is associated with other-direction, the individual sees himself as the servant of his fellow man. Regardless of the identity-sense, the difference between puritan and non-puritan societies can be seen in what those societies produce. Germany and the United States, both of which have moved from a puritan inner- to a puritan other-direction, concentrate upon *quantity*. Denmark and Sweden, both of which have moved from a non-puritan inner- to a random-direction, have concentrated upon *quality*. Even though the latter are welfare states—and therefore committed to quantity in distribution—they are deeply attentive to taste and design in most of the things they make.

Differences Between Puritan and Non-Puritan Peoples

As we look back, we cannot help being struck by the difference between puritan peoples and non-puritans. The more puritan a nation, the less original and creative it has been. The less puritan its people, the more creative and innovative. It is significant that the Greeks, who were the most individualistic and the least puritan, were also the most creative. It is also significant that the Romans were among the least creative. It has been said of both the Romans and the Japanese that they never invented anything—that their genius was for imitation. What is more likely is that their capacity for adaptation and exploitation has been a mark of their puritanism.

Puritanism can be thought of as discouraging individualism because it teaches the individual to think of himself as a means, and as being subordinate to a larger purpose. This is not necessarily the case, however. It has been so in Japan, but that country was never individualistic; its puritanism began in a feudal and corporate society. It was not so in the protestant West at a time when the West was individualistic. In fact, the height of puritanism came at a time when individualism was at *its* height. Adam Smith captured the spirit of each in his theology, where *laissez faire* was formalized. Smith's entrepreneurial system brought man his greatest individual responsibility. It saw the highest productivity as coming from a society of individuals set free under God. The controls that an organic society would have had to impose could not possibly have encouraged the output of time and effort that came from *laissez faire.*

Whether he is puritan or not, man's individuality and his expression of it become stylized with the passage of time. The artist's work loses its simplicity and wonder. It turns from the joy of self-discovery to an exaltation over the discovery and mastery of nature. As even this triumph becomes a thing of the past, the artist becomes more engrossed with his work. He becomes increasingly concerned with the medium, and less with the message. He becomes a perfectionist, and strives for technical excellence. He is no longer only a free spirit; he is a master as well.

The Identity Cycle in Ancient Greece

To show how individualism has once before dissolved into collectivism, I shall trace the transition in ancient Greece and Rome. In both cases the change began with a questioning of customs, manners, and morals. In both cases it led to an abandonment of the transcendent symbols and deities that had given meaning and identity to the people. Greece's transition from tribalism to inner-direction began in the middle of the ninth century and ended in the middle of the sixth. This was the Golden Age. By 546 Greek religion had become institutionalized, and the threat of Persian invasion was leading the people to become as nearly nationalized as they were ever to be. Within a hundred years the wealth and leisure of the upper classes had encouraged the flowering of art and philosophy. It had brought the sophistry that questioned the respectability of the gods and the responsibility of men. Still a hundred years later, in the fourth century, Plato attributed the failure of Greek culture to the evil frame of mind of the sophists, who had spread the notion that might is right. He attacked the immorality of individuals who take all they can from life without regard for other people's share—and with no concern for the future.[2] These people were not individualists in the sense that we have used the term. They now had no point of reference outside of themselves. They were already random-directed.

In the second century, when Rome was going through the same identity crisis, the Senators decreed that no philosopher might come into the city. Although they knew, as we do, that many causes—like war, taxation, unemployment, and family instability—were contributing to the erosion of personhood, they recognized the need to maintain moral and social tradition. Will Durant tells us, of the pedants whom they banned,

> Few of these Greek teachers had religious beliefs; fewer transmitted any; a small minority of them followed Epicurus . . . in describing religion as the chief evil in life.[3]

The identity crisis of the Greeks and the Romans was the same as our own. The first symptoms were those that welled up out of the social unconscious—a protracted period of wars whose issues were too large to understand. Then followed the conscious revolt against the old standards and the old means of expressing personhood. In our case the process began with World War I. Then came dada art, intellectual subjectivism, and anarchic theology. Finally the social fabric itself began to fall apart, with the individual's claim of emancipation from obligation to society, and from the standards by which societies have always preserved their identity.

In Greece this process began with the Peloponnesian wars—a series of almost continuing conflicts that lasted from 431 to 404. It continued with a failure in religion and art, and with their replacement by science and philos-

A Cycle of Non-puritan Social Personality

Age	Century	Movements	Government	Statesmen	Artists	Intellectuals	Social Identity
Heroic (before 850)	12th	Settling of Greece	Tribal				Corporate
	10th	Migrations, foreign trade	Monarchies				Transition to
	9th	Rise of city-states	"				Inner-direction
Golden (850-546)	8th	Aristocrats take power	Oligarchies		Homer		"
	7th	Political & economic expansion	"				"
		Social imbalance & injustice	"		Hesiod		"
		Occasional tyrannies	Oligarchies & tyrannies	Dracon			Individualism
	6th	War-leagues of city-states	"	Solon	Sappho		"
		Popular religious cults	"	Pisistratus			"
		Sacred wars	"				"
		Codes of law, judicial reform					
Age of Grandeur (546-466)		Persian capture of Asian colonies	"				"
	5th	Extension of democracy	Democracy	Themistocles			
		Ostracism: protection from tyrants	"	Aristides	Pindar		
		Wars of Persian imperialism	"	Leonidas	Aeschylus		
		Shifting hegemonies of city-states	"	Pericles	Phidias	Anaxagoras	Transition to
Identity Crisis (466-404)		Introduction of philosophy & atheism	"	Alcibiades	Aristophanes	Thucydides	Random-direction
		Civil wars, esp. Peloponnesian	"	Epaminondas	Euripides	Socrates	"
	4th	Failure of democracy	Anarchy & tyranny	Xenophon	Demosthenes	Plato	Random-direction
Age of Failure (after 404)		Rise of Macedonia	Autocracy	Philip	Praxiteles	Aristotle	"
		Macedonian imperialism	Imperial	Alexander		Isocrates	"
	3rd	Conquest by Syria	"				
	2nd	Conquest by Rome	"				Collectivism

Individualism began with the transfer of power from princes to nobles. It ended when power—already having reached the lower classes—became abstracted from personal responsibility. Note that philosophy flowered only after the decline of religion had brought political power to an end, and after an identity crisis had degraded the quality of art. Philosophy explained the failure of power and identity, but was unable to restore it. After the third century, Greek individualism could be used only in a catalysis of Roman culture.

ophy. The resulting end of Greek inner-direction is described by Cecil Lavell:

> The mental restlessness of the fourth century was not due to
> any one man any more than was its moral and political failure.
> It sprang on the one hand from a sort of anxiety and nervous
> discontent, from the passing of old faiths and the feverish
> grasping at new ones that were elusive and debatable; on the
> other hand from gossip and diversity and shifting contacts of
> trade, travel and war.[4]

It can be said of all wars of social crisis that they not
only are an expression of that crisis, but tend greatly to
intensify it. This was as true of the ancient world as it is
today. N. G. L. Hammond says this of the Athenians in
this period:

> While sophistry was a solvent of traditional belief, the influ-
> ences of war tended in the same direction. The evacuation of
> Attica, the terrors of the plague, and the disaster at Syracuse
> loosened the strands of religious belief, and the rigors of war
> and defeat made some men question the right of the state to
> make such demands. Philosophy, too, having defined its cos-
> mogony and disposed of any deity, turned to man as the
> microcosm and studied his personal psychology. The shift of
> interest from the group to the individual upset the traditional
> relation between the state and the citizen.[5]

It is remarkable that Greek individualism, even in its
death throes, never succumbed to the temptation to be
collectivized. We can appreciate this if we trace Greek
random-direction from its beginnings down to the end of
the city-state culture. The transition to random-direction
began in the time of Pericles, Athens' greatest statesman,
who died in the first years of the great Peloponnesian War.
It was Pericles who presided over the building of the
Parthenon and other glories of the Acropolis. He was a
contemporary of Greece's greatest creative minds—Pindar,
Sophocles, Phidias, Herodotus, and Euripides. The chief
influence upon this generation was Pericles' own coun-
selor, Anaxagoras, who taught a mechanical theory of a
material universe that had been set in motion by an irrevo-
cable act. This did not deny the possibility of a God whom

the Greeks had never known, but it demolished the pantheon of gods whom they had worshipped. It envisioned a Fate man could never know, and which was unconcerned with human love and justice. Along with Anaxagoras' physics there arose the ethical thought of Protagoras and the sophists. Each of these contributed to a crisis in Greek identity, and consequently to random-direction. Anaxagoras and Protagoras were the Marx and Freud of the ancient world. It was largely because of them that the generation after Pericles had to fight the Peloponnesian War.

Two generations later, when Macedonian power was bringing an end to Greek democracy, there was an impulse to collectivize. Yet it was too weak to be a stimulus to action. The only prominent Greek who favored panhellenic organization was the Athenian, Isocrates. He alone saw the need for a unifying act to preserve the Grecian character. He was opposed by Demosthenes, who, for all his gifts as an orator, had the unwisdom of the random-directed—and a flair for demagoguery as well. Demosthenes conjured up the ghosts of all the mini-nationalisms of the past, and Greece went down without a fight. Philip of Macedonia turned out to be only the first of many foreign rulers.

The Identity Cycle of Ancient Rome

Rome's cycle of identity was an entirely different one. It differed because of the puritan ethic, and because of the type of social personality that puritanism provides. When, in the first century before Christ, the Roman Republic was nearing its end, the people were ready for an empire ruled by tyrants. They had been other-directed for several hundred years, and were already in the midst of a transition to random-direction. In the century before Augustus there had been a continuing identity crisis. There had been civil wars, occasional rule by tyrants, and a continuing social revolution. Three times—in 135, 103, and 73—the Romans had had to fight armies of rebellious slaves. The size of these rebellions is shown in that it took a total of nine years to put them down. The last servile war—that of Spartacus and his gladiators—saw two Roman armies decimated before the slaves were overcome.

Rome's puritanism made it natural that when the ancient world was ripe for collectivism, Rome should become its master. The other imperial nations had not been able both to conquer and to rule. The Persian rule was short-lived because its people were collectivists without ever having been inner-directed. They did not have the ingenuity and resourcefulness to direct the lives of others. Like the Russians and Chinese today, their power was largely in their numbers, not to mention their cruelty and inhumanity. The Macedonian conquest was doomed because Alexander's men were individualists without ever having been puritan. Like the British after them, they were able by sheer boldness and tenacity to dominate nations whose people numbered many times their own. But they could not keep their conquests. They did not care about ruling, and they were not impersonal enough to use the necessary force.

The Romans were able both to conquer and to rule. They had been individualists, and they were spurred on by a drive to excel. They did not, like the Greeks, limit their population by practicing infanticide and gericide, and by using sex for pleasure. They did not, like the Greeks, emphasize the individual citizen's liberties. Rather, they emphasized his responsibilities—both to the family and the state. The early Romans put a puritan emphasis upon chastity in women and upon the martial virtues in men. Rome was a Sparta raised to a national—and finally to an international—scale.

The similarity of Rome's cycle of identity with our own is so remarkable that we can show it here without any preliminaries. (By our cycle I mean that of the puritan West.) This begins in northern Europe with the rise of unrelated associations. It is translated to the United States with emigration of puritans both from Britain and the continent. For us, of course, the cycle is not completed. We are left to speculate on what may lie ahead.

A Recurring Cycle of Social Identity in Ancient Rome and the Modern West

Social Identity	Form of Government	Ancient Rome	Modern West
Corporate identity	Chief & council	-753 B.C.	-A.D. 1100
Transition to inner-direction	Absolute monarchy	753	1100
Inner-direction	Constitutional monarchy	616	1215
Transition to other-direction	Constitutional democracy	509	1776
Other-direction	Absolute democracy	123	1935
Transition to random-direction	Universal state	31	?
Random-direction	Destruction of empire	410 A.D.	?
Transition to corporate identity	Feudal system	887	?

Key to dates:	Ancient Rome	Modern West
Transition (inner)	753 Founding of Rome	1100 Rise of Towns
Inner-direction	616 Kings elected by Senate	1215 Magna Carta
Transition (other)	509 Founding of Republic	1776 American Revolution
Other-direction	123 Gracchian reforms	1935 U.S Wealth-tax Act
Transition (random)	31 Establishment of Empire	
Random-direction	410 Fall of Rome	
Transition (corporate)	887 Dissolution of Charlemagne's empire	

Lacking surer clues to the dates of change in social personality, we are here tying them to the dates that signify a change in the popular base for authority in government. This method can be questioned; forms of government are not always linked with the forms of social identity shown here. Nevertheless the forms of government do give an indication as to where power resides, and as to people's concept of their identification with the group. The causes of transition from one form of social identity to another were the same in Rome as they have been in the modern West. Corporality turned to individuality because of the multiplying of unrelated associations. Inner-direction turned to other-direction because the multiplying of symbols and values destroyed men's ability to depend upon a single set of givens. Other-direction turned to random-direction because men lost the power to act responsibly, and because they could not acknowledge an obligation to society. As each cycle of identity evolved, authority for government moved to successively broader segments of society. It reached its limit in the state that is referred to here as "absolute democracy." From this point on, authority tended to dissolve rather than to be distributed more widely.

The Politics of Collective Personality

It is a paradox of social order that centralized government is made necessary only by the disappearance of
individual identity. When men regard themselves as free
and accountable they are less concerned with society's
obligation to them than they are with their obligation to
society. Even where there is widespread poverty there is
little apathy. The society can count upon its members'
concern for those around them. Where the individual's
maturity is not assumed, the reverse is true. Not only is the
individual regarded as free from obligation to society; even
the family is relieved from fulfilling its function. At this
point it is the state that becomes the *paterfamilias*. This is
the point where fidelity and devotion come to an end, and
where bread and circuses begin. It is the point where men
surrender their responsibility for their private lives as well
as for the republic. Arnold Toynbee has commented on
the process:

> One of the most conspicuous marks of disintegration . . . is a
> phenomenon in the last stage but one of the decline and fall,
> when a disintegrating civilization purchases a reprieve by sub-
> mitting to forcible political unification in a universal state.[6]

Such unification seems right and good to members of a
disintegrating society. The collectivist sees the only real
order as being a universal one. He submits to unification,
not so much out of a sense of weakness as in the belief
that it is the only just social order.

When the Roman Republic came to an end the people
were ready for tyranny. They did not question their rulers'
right to rule. They had, for some generations, been neo-
tribalists. A swing to random-direction was not long in
coming. Even in Augustus' time Rome was having serious
problems with social identity. The family was already an
outworn institution. Sex was no longer identified with life,
and sexual fidelity no longer mattered. As an illustration,
it was amusingly recalled that Julius Caesar had been a
husband to every wife in Rome—and a wife to every
husband. The Romans' pleasures distracted them from
sterner duties. Augustus had such difficulty finding re-

cruits for his legions that he had to hire mercenaries from the conquered nations. The result was that power was transferred from the aristocrats to the soldiery. What power was left to Rome itself was held by the rabble—and by the demagogues who controlled it. With the exception of a few conscientious administrations, such as that of Marcus Aurelius, the age of the Empire was one of growing personal chaos. By the beginning of the third century even public power had begun to fail. The glory of imperial Rome lay only in technical competence. This was partly due to an accumulation of knowledge and partly due to the inertia that maintained the puritan ethic. The failure of individual power led, in the third century, to economic and political collapse. By the fourth century even intellectual power had disappeared, save in the Christian Church.

What was true of the Empire as a whole was especially true of the cities. Even in Augustus' time the cities had not been safe to live in. Poverty and crime went hand in hand with the new random-direction, and with men's inability to deal with reality. Bread and circuses were more than an indulgence; they soon became a necessity. The continuing trend to personal irresponsibility is suggested in a remark of Lewis Mumford's. It refers to the year 430:

> When the Vandals were hammering at the gates of Hippo, Augustine's city, the groans of the dying defenders on the wall mingled with the roar of the spectators in the circus, more concerned with their day's enjoyment than with even their ultimate personal safety.[7]

Group Guilt and the Mystery Cults

Even in cultural decay, however, men pay attention to cause and effect. They cannot disregard their intuitions concerning justice and order. While they may dodge their private responsibilities, they cannot ignore society's failures. Consequently, there arises an impulse to find a culprit. Since individual accountability has already been discounted, blame must be placed upon particular classes and peoples, and upon society as a whole. This happened in Rome, even as it is happening now. It was manifested in a mounting sense of group guilt and in a neurotic inability to deal with personal and social responsibility.

The chief evidence of this neuroticism lies in the proliferation of the mystery cults that sprang up at this time. These offered their devotees a cleansing from group guilt through expiatory rites that involved shedding the blood of a vicarious victim. They offered a return to personhood by a saving relationship with a "personal" god. Christianity was akin to these mystery cults, and it was in it that the answer to guilt was found. The Church's protection of personhood saved the ancient West from total extinction, and secured the seed of identity for a far-off renaissance.

Let us consider the scene at Rome, as social identity changed from other- to random-direction. The dividing line was the turn of the Christian era. The three centuries before Christ had been a time of an increasing other-direction. The ancient gods had lost all influence by this time. Philosophy had showed that they were only the personification of the forces of nature. They had never laid down any ethical absolutes; consequently Roman inner-direction had not lasted for long. In these three centuries philosophy absorbed men's ethical and religious thought. Stoicism kept the upper classes attentive to their civic duty. It called them to set examples of Spartan simplicity. Epicureanism flourished among the middle classes, especially in the century before Christ. It was a philosophy of pleasure that led to the hedonism of later Rome. The middle classes learned to reconcile the epicure with the puritan in the same way that we, today, reconcile luxury in consumption with puritanism in production.

Rome's earliest random-direction was concerned with the rights of the individual. As with the G.I. prisoners in Korea, the basic question was not, "What can I do to help myself?" but "What can be done to help me?" The old sense of public obligation disappeared. Intellectual subjectivism replaced the earlier curiosity and resourcefulness. The Roman populace became politically limp. It had already lost its orientation, and now it lost its nerve. Inevitably, the Empire soon became unable to defend itself, and a feeling of malaise began to permeate the people. A new factor came upon the scene—group guilt. It led to a multiplicity of mystery cults and to centuries of self-recrimination. From the very beginning, the Christians were the most obvious scapegoats. Nero had accused them of starting the fire, and in time they were blamed for the failure of the culture. Yet, even when their blood was joined with that of the animal sacrifices, they never accepted the burden of corporate guilt. St. Augustine's treatise, *The City of God*, was their reply to the contention that Christ had brought about the downfall of Rome.

Return of Personal Religion

One thing that the mystery religions accomplished was to restore a sense of personhood. Philosophy—which looked upon ignorance and suffering as the chief evils in life—had proved too impersonal to meet the needs of man. The cults of Isis, Cybele, and Mithras faced a failure that was both personal and deliberate. While they were only make-believe religions, they redirected man's attention to his own perversity. They offered his society a promise of forgiveness and salvation. They not only relieved group guilt, but they reaffirmed the fact of human responsibility.

As we look back, we can see that the old Greco-Roman culture had to die to prove the falsity of its assumptions—that there is no God against whom one can sin, and that the chief evils of man's experience must therefore be ignorance and suffering. It was only by the Empire's dissolution in a universal impersonality that men could be personal once more. That death took the culture with it, but it left Western man ready for a rebirth that was to come when the time was ripe.

At the point where his guilt ceased to bind man to a life without hope, the possibility for a cultural rebirth came into being. This was the point where a *real* mystery religion pointed anew to the theme that primitive man always knew—the theme of a personal relationship between a Creator God and a being who is made in His image; the theme of a relationship that is damaged by sin, but restored by forgiveness and grace.

The modern West is fortunate to have, in its identity crisis, something more than the historical example of the ancient world. It has a God who has always proved stronger than the gods that men create in their emerging years, and stronger than the philosophies they construct for their years of decline. If it will use them, the West has the symbols and values that originated in Judaism and that were carried over into Christianity. These are, and always have been, adequate to a culture's needs, and at any point in its cycle.

Nevertheless, reality itself is meaningless to men who will not perceive it. Without being objectively aware of that reality, the West seems to be doomed to a repetition of the Greco-Roman cycle. The only possibility that can be imagined—aside from a more gracious intervention of the Spirit—is that some catastrophe like a Deluge or a nuclear holocaust will once more give a *personal* meaning to the history of man. When men build a Tower of Babel they can be brought to their senses only when that tower is thrown to the ground.

Notes on Chapter Five:

1. N. G. L. Hammond, *A History of Greece* (Oxford: Oxford University Press, 1959), p. 67.

2. G. B. Grundy, *A History of the Greek and Roman World* (New York: R. V. Coleman, c. 1925), pp. 237f.

3. Will Durant, *Caesar and Christ* (New York: Simon and Schuster, 1944), p. 95.

4. Cecil F. Lavell, *A Biography of the Greek People* (Boston: Houghton Mifflin, 1934), p. 183.

5. N. G. L. Hammond, *A History of Greece* (Oxford: Oxford University Press, 1959), pp. 421f.

6. Arnold Toynbee, *A Study of History* (D. C. Somervell's abridgment) (New York: Dell, 1965), I, 286.
York: McGraw-Hill, 1966), p. 90.

7. Lewis Mumford, *The City in History* (New York: Harcourt, Brace & World, 1961), p. 230.

A Cycle of Social and Individual Power

Social Identity	*Form of Government*	*Social and Individual Power in Relation to Tribal State*		
Corporate	Chief and Council	Minus		Plus
Transition	Absolute Monarchy		Social Power →	Individual Power ↓
Inner-directed	Constitutional Monarchy	Puritan Ethic Begins		
Transition	Constitutional Democracy	Decay in Transcendent Symbols		
Other-directed	Absolute Democracy	Symbols Gone, Identity Crisis		
Transition	Universal Dictatorship	Puritan Ethic Ends		
Random-directed	Dissolving Empire			
Transition	Feudal System			
Corporate	Chief and Council			

Individual power is measured by those qualities that enable the individual to act freely and responsibly: conscience, convictions, secure values, initiative, resourcefulness, variety of experiences and skills, ability to find satisfaction in achievements.

Social power is measured by those qualities that indicate achievement by the group: organizational abilities, group motivations, leadership skills, accumulation of wealth and technology, with ability to work with superior force.

Note that at all points in the cycle the trend in social power lags behind that in individual power. In early stages, with technology and wealth only beginning to expand, the society can only be as strong as its members have already become. A will to power must precede the capacity for power.

In later stages the power of society as a whole will increase even though an identity crisis has caused its citizens' psychic power to diminish. This is largely from inertia. Wealth, technology and organizational skills will continue to give social power even after a populace has become politically limp.

Eventually, in the tribal state, social and individual power again become equal.

Chapter Six

A DELINEATION
OF ABSOLUTES

The system of ethics that has, among other things, been called The New Morality and Situation Ethics is not a new system. It is as old as the random-direction with which it is associated. It is based on the presumption that there are no moral absolutes. It is preferred by those who hold that right conduct can be determined only existentially. Because of their mental orientation, such people cannot see the propriety of universal rules. For them it is enough that each situation be approached with honesty, good intentions, and an open mind.

Most situationists of the past have been atheists or agnostics. They have asserted with good logic that there can be no absolute values unless there is an Absolute Person. They have also maintained that since moral judgments are personal they must be tailored to the needs of the persons involved. Situationists find offense in the solutions that flow from the science of casuistry. This is a study that systematizes moral choice, that offers advance opinions on how we should react to particular ethical situations. To situationists, casuistry calls for stupid obedience, not for moral choice.

Now that random-direction is becoming a form of *social* identity, situation ethics has enlisted a following it never had before. It provides a pattern for religious as well as irreligious people. This includes those who believe in a personal God, but who cannot accept the existence of an absolute Law governing man.

Situation ethics recognizes only one absolute—the obligation to love. Since it rejects the applicability of *Thou shalt nots*, it becomes the only possible ethic for men of good will whose orientation is random-direction. Fortunately, it meets their wants. It is existential rather than universal, person-oriented rather than value-oriented. It does not inhibit feelings and desire, but rather transforms them into what is "positive" and "fulfilling." One of the advantages claimed for it is that it is not necessarily a Christian system, and is therefore open to all men of good will.

Christians who have espoused situation ethics have pressed the point that, since love is the fulfilling of the law,* the new system is a sufficient one. They believe that it is the one practical system in a world where the old absolutes have disappeared, and where change is the only constant. They point out that situation ethics has something the old casuistry lacked; it refuses to give oracular pre-judgments. In this it conforms to the requirements of a Jean-Paul Sartre, who says, "No general ethics can tell you what is to be done; there are no omens in the world."[1]

The Weaknesses of Situation Ethics

There are a number of weaknesses in situation ethics, however. In absolutizing only love, and in leaving justice in limbo, it fails to meet the deepest human needs. When we find that men are angry over some injustice, it is usually because they have been deprived of their *rights*—and not because others have withheld their love.

Secondly, situation ethics is not practical. Those who have never been trained to obey the Law can hardly be expected to be obedient to love. Love is blind and easily abused. Its misuse hurts people even more than does the misuse of law. We may observe that those who have not been schooled in the Law are often seeking its discipline,

*Romans 13:10

even when they seem to be trying to find out how much they can get away with. I doubt whether many troubled youngsters really want to find the "law for themselves," which is the objective of random-directed man. What they seem to want, rather, is a justice that can be spelled out in universal authoritative terms. I believe that a great deal of delinquent behavior can be traced to the subconscious impulse of young people to seek punishment, as a situational and nonverbal way of finding out what the rules are.

Paul Tillich has drawn our attention to a psychological factor that makes a love ethic a difficult one at best. He says,

> Emotions cannot be demanded. We cannot demand them of ourselves. If we try, something artificial is produced which shows the traits of what is to be suppressed in its production. Repentance, intentionally produced, hides self-complacency in perversion. Love, intentionally produced, shows indifference or hostility in perversion.[2]

Sir Walter Moberly supports this point with an observation of his own:

> The distinctively Christian morality of grace, in which "charity" or "love" is the chief motive-force, cannot be the basis for the rules of a semi-Christian society. . . . The communal rules cannot embody standards higher than will gain the approval of the average decent man; they must express the morality of law rather than the morality of grace.[3]

Its Absolutism

Actually, we can make a good case that situation ethics is not a *relative* ethic at all. If we consider the semantics rather than the arguments, we find that the situationist's love and the absolutist's law are virtually the same thing. The absolutist holds that *there are values that are intrinsic in the human situation*. The situationist is saying that *there are no intrinsic values apart from the human situation*. In essence, both are saying the same thing. The situationist has become an absolutist because, in order to have an ethic, he has had to absolutize *love*. He has also had to absolutize another virtue—the one that shows the proof of love. That virtue is *the obligation of taking responsible action*. This, however, is Law. It is the old obedience spelled in a new way. Situation ethics may be seen as a system for people who have never been conditioned by the *no-noes* of childhood training to take a universal view of private ethics.

A final difficulty with situation ethics is that it is appropriate only for the early phases of random-direction. It is helpful to those who have broken with traditional values and symbols, and who have therefore to approach each moral situation anew. But it says nothing to those who are so burdened with group guilt that the only out seems to lie in the occult or in new mystery cults.

Its Uniqueness

What situation ethics does say to people in all times and places is that each particular situation requires a unique moral choice. Every judgment must reconcile a variety of claims, such as those of mercy and justice, of short- and long-range satisfactions, of greater and lesser responsibilities. Each of these can be regarded as an absolute; the only relativity is the question of where, in man's judgment, it comes out in its conflict with the others. When one's obedience is only to a casuistical system, one is not altogether making a present choice. One is choosing to be consistent with a past choice. In addition, one is preferring the judgment that someone else has made—someone who could not be aware of the situations into which his judgment might be pressed. It can be argued that one who chooses such a system is preferring rectitude to righteousness.

Despite these valuable insights situation ethics cannot stand by itself. It is a transitory pattern for morality, even as random-direction is a transitional form of identity. Because random-direction is polytheistic, situation ethics is polytheistic; it rejects the possibility of a unifying pattern of law.

Unfortunately, in settling for a situation ethic, the random-directed man is not demonstrating an understanding of freedom. He is only showing his inability to live with paradox. The situationist can accept only love as an absolute. The traditionalist can accept the universality both of love and of law. He is a "legalist" only if he values law more highly than love—only if, for him, the demands of justice seem to preclude the possibility of mercy.

Its View of History

A final observation on situation ethics is that it takes a random-directed view of history as well as of morality. It has the same view of freedom that led Tolstoy to call the free man's history "a tissue of disconnected accidents." This view is not one of freedom. Rather, it is one of bondage. It does not describe the life of man, but of animals. To the lower creatures, life can only be a tissue of unrelated events. By contrast, man sees all things as being ultimately related. He perceives that ultimately all things are connected to the One who has given them their substance and shape.

The Priority of Law

If we are to understand what moral absolutes are, we must give our attention to Law rather than to love. It is true that love is the only means by which the Law is fulfilled. Law, however, will always be the description of what the fulfilment is. When Paul described love as the fulfilment of the Law, he appeared to be suggesting that the Law had served its purpose and could henceforth be disregarded. In speaking of the Law as a schoolmaster bringing man to perfection, he seemed to treat it as the primary stage of a rocket—something that can be discarded when the rocket is in orbit. This is an inadequate interpretation, and it is not supported by Christ's own words. Jesus did not release even the perfect man from the Law's obligations.* What he did was to highlight the absolute in

*Luke 17:10

an imperative that successive generations of Jews had reduced to a situation ethic,

> Think not that I am come to destroy the Law . . . I am come
> not to destroy, but to fulfil.*

He went on to say,

> Verily I say unto you, Till heaven and earth pass, one jot or
> one tittle shall in no wise pass from the Law, till all be fulfilled.†

Men have always had difficulties with the idea of divine
Law. It has seemed to be the fiat of a capricious deity who
is bent upon dominating his creatures. It has seemed to
make them puppets. The first impulse of most men is to
say "No" to such a god. But the God who is discernible in
the biblical revelation is not despotic. Neither is the Law
that He has given. The Law is no less than the minimum
description of the perfect man. It is the yardstick against
which all men are to be measured. As Paul Tillich put it,
"The Law is man's essential nature, put against him as
law."[4]

The purpose of the law is not to block achievement, but
rather to fulfil it. Even though it is the standard by which
men may judge themselves, it is not intended primarily to
show a man how far short of perfection he is. It is to reveal
how much he has yet to grow, and in what directions.

Ethical Absolutes in the Bible

For a delineation of ethical absolutes we must refer to
the Bible. Even there, we must discriminate between what
is divine and what is human, between what is absolute and
what is situational. The Bible is not uniformly inspired,
and it is not, therefore, uniformly authoritative. The Law
and the Prophets convey the sense of an ethical absolute
far better than do the Writings and the Apocrypha of the
Old Testament. The Gospels convey the sense of absolute
better than do the New Testament Epistles. The later

*Matt. 5:17 (AV)
†Matt. 5:18 (AV)

writings of both testaments are in large part a humanizing of what was too absolute for their respective communities to live comfortably with. This means that, in respect to the *quality* of the Law, the line of demarcation is not between the Old Testament and the New, but between the Law, the Prophets, and the Gospels on the one hand, and the Writings, the Apocrypha, and the Epistles on the other. The one are absolute and the other are situational.

The Jews of Jesus' time were quite aware of this watering down of the absolute. To them, the Law and the Prophets stood first, then came the Writings. As for the Apocrypha, it had been written in a profane language— Greek. In addition, it had been written long years after the spirit of prophecy had departed from Israel; therefore they could not regard it as divinely inspired. It was only an embodiment of sound ethical wisdom.

A similar comparison may be made between the Gospels and the Epistles of the New Testament. In their attempt to give a practical application to Jesus' teachings and commandments, the epistolers fell far short of the divine imperative that appears in the Gospels. Except for the letters attributed to John, the Epistles show almost uniformly a reduction of the Gospel Law.

We find an illustration in the biblical command to give to the needy—something proclaimed with equal force by Moses and Christ. In neither the Law nor the Gospel is almsgiving linked with the promise of reward. Rather, it is linked with the goodness that God has shown in the past: Israel is indebted to the Lord for all that it is and has. Therefore, the Israelite's obedience in sharing his substance with the poor is God's way of showing His compassion for the poor, *whom He also loves.*

By contrast with this imperative, the Writings and the Apocrypha—in proportion to the lateness of their authorship—never speak of almsgiving without referring to "what's in it for the giver."* In the same way, Jesus'

Compare Deut. 15:11,14,15 with Prov. 11:25; Sirach 12:2; Tobit 4:7-9 commandments of unselfish love are twisted by the epistolers into reminders of the benefits to be obtained.

The Christian can see in the Gospels more than a recovery of the sense of absolute manifested by Moses. He can see a heightening of that absolute, and a stripping away of all that is situational. For all their engaging simplicity, Jesus' teachings are absolute *in toto.* This is true whether they are considered as manifestations of Law or of love. While they were clothed with the simple and homely vesture of Palestinian life, they are true for all times and places. Their dramatic intensity, their congruency with human experience, and their witness to a life of intimacy with the Father—all point to a unique intrusion of the divine into the human that led His hearers to proclaim, "Jesus is God."

Jesus' Clarification of Law

The uniqueness of the Gospel imperative is shown in that Jesus did not hesitate to judge the Law of Moses. In so doing, He seemed to set Himself above the Law—a thing that would make Him equal with God. This, of course, is why Jesus was put to death. But Jesus did not intend to set Himself above the Law; His own words are witness to that. What He did was to speak with an authority higher than Moses', to show what was situational in the Law that *Moses* gave.

An example of Jesus' heightening of the Law of Moses is shown in Mark 10:2-9. A group of pharisees had come to Jesus, soliciting His views on the Hebrew law of divorce (Deut. 24:1-4). They may have hoped for an answer that would align Jesus with the conservative school of Shammai or the liberal school of Hillel. But Jesus would not be trapped in a situational concern. He referred back to the Law itself, asking the pharisees, "What did Moses *command* you?" They replied, in effect, "Moses *permitted* us to divorce our wives." Their answer was in itself an ac-

---

*Compare Matt. 10:8b; 25:40; Mark 8:35-37; Luke 14:11-14 with
  Gal. 6:9,10; Eph. 6:8; Phil. 4:17; Heb. 6:10

knowledgment that this point of the Law was a precept of men, and not a divine commandment. Jesus then pointed to the absolute behind this precept. He said, in effect, "Moses gave you this situation ethic because you were hardhearted. But in the beginning, when God created male and female (and before Moses gave you the "law"), no such precept existed. In creating male and female, God also created the family. He established a pattern for human community, and it is a pattern that cannot be broken. *What therefore God hath joined together, let not man put asunder.*"

Law Internalized in the Spirit

Jesus' clarifying of the Law of Moses included other dimensions than family relation, and other aspects than behavior. The most vivid of His absolutizings are those of the Sermon on the Mount. Here Jesus said,

> You have learnt how it was said to our ancestors: *You must not kill;* and if anyone does kill he must answer for it before the court. But I say this to you: anyone who is angry with his brother will answer for it before the court. . . . You have learnt how it was said: *You must not commit adultery.* But I say this to you: if a man looks at a woman lustfully, he has already committed adultery with her in his heart.*

Here we are referred back from external behavior to motivation. We return to what was earlier described as the most critical factor in identity—memory, imagination and intention. Apart from inner intentions, the Law means little. A man who obeys the Law without a good intention cannot be said to fulfil it. Not-to-kill, not-to-steal, and not-to-commit-adultery are indeed a preservative for society. But the purpose of the Law is to create perfect men. The one who gives outward obedience to the Law, while keeping greed and lust in his heart, becomes a greedy and lustful man. Moreover, because these things cannot be bottled up, they are bound to have a corrosive effect on those who are

---

*Matt. 5:21,22,27,28 (Jerusalem Bible)

around. The woman who is lusted after is bound to know it. Even without willing it, she is likely to make an artful response. Her imagination may become so inflamed, and the coals of old memories raked over so subtly, that her own integrity and that of her family are threatened.

The same is even more true of anger. With age, the desires of the world and the flesh are likely to decrease. But anger, envy, and pride increase with the passage of time, and are an ever growing threat against the soul. The perfecting of the disposition is made possible only by paying attention to the most difficult of all Jesus' absolutes,

> Ye have heard that it hath been said, Thou shalt love thy neighbor, and hate thine enemy. But I say unto you, Love your enemies, bless them that curse you, do good to them that hate you, and pray for them which despitefully use you, and persecute you; that ye may be the children of your Father which is in heaven.*

There is an undeniable reason for paying attention to these commandments. A mild and forgiving attitude is the only one that allows injustice to be forgotten in a world where the best of men do a great deal of harm. To forgive is to forget. It is to be emptied of anger—and thus to grow up in the pattern of the Law. To say "No" to lust is to be freed from what, uncurbed, can lead to all manner of vice. To be free from lust is to meet the deepest needs, not only of women and children, but of men as well. It makes possible the perfection of individuals and families and of society at large. To know this is to know that manliness and brutishness are very different things.

Greek and Hebrew Mind-Sets

To get a firm grasp of moral absolutes, it is first necessary to understand the people who first were aware of them—the Hebrews. We can best understand the Hebrew mentality when we compare it with the gentile mind,

*Matt. 5:43-45 (AV)

whose highest flowering was that of Greek thought. The Greek mind is analytical, given to separation and subdivision. The Hebrew mind is holistic. It synthesizes the data it deals with, looking for relations in unity. Greek thought is static. Its key words are nouns. Its concern is with space, form, and structure. Its communication is chiefly visual. Hebrew thought is dynamic. Its chief words are verbs. Its primary dimension is that of time rather than space.

The Greek's talent was that of understanding and molding the exterior world. He developed the arts, the sciences, and the humanities. The Hebrew's world was a moral and spiritual one. To him, religion and history were one. The Greek, by contrast, cannot relate spirit and matter. Faced with evil and injustice, he must resort to philosophy or mythology. The Hebrew is an incarnationalist. He sees flesh and spirit as interpenetrating one another, even though the enfleshment is temporary. For him, the created order becomes the arena for hammering out the moral issues of life. Life has a historic, as well as a dramatic purpose. In Greek thought, man's life has neither beginning nor ending. Cyclical patterns of nature and of history have value chiefly in the chance they give for worldly gain. In Hebrew thought the only important cycle is a spiritual one. It is that of a gift misused, followed by punishment, repentance, amendment, and restoration. Hebrew thought is centered in the Creator, and Greek thought in the creation. For the Hebrew, character comes from the wise use of responsibility; for the Greek, it comes from the uses of freedom.

Singularity of the Hebrews

We can make three further observations about the Hebrew himself, to distinguish him from all other peoples. First is his remarkable passion for life. His is a vitality that values the good not only for his own generation, but for the furthest generation as well. Second is the Hebrew's remarkable sense of unity and harmony in creation. Third is the urgent sense of a divine imperative that underlies the requirements of ethical behavior. This springs from the absolute demands of a God who has charged all of creation with the power of his personality.

The greatest force in the ethical Law is the personhood of God. The Old Testament does not know God as "the man upstairs." It cannot take God thus lightly. Nor dare it speak of Him impersonally as "the ground of being." This means that *holiness* and *righteousness* cannot be separated as, in gentile thought, they so frequently are. Holiness—which is a state of identification with God—may seem to have little to do with righteousness—which is the mark of ethical behavior. Yet, in the Hebrew mind the two are inextricably linked. There is no holiness without righteousness, and there is no righteousness without holiness. Their unity lies in this: that both originate in the mind of God. God accepts a man as righteous because his goodness is motivated by reverence and love for God. God accepts a man as holy because in his attendance upon the divine Person he does not neglect the persons of men.

Apart from this unity, there is a wide difference between the two. Righteousness belongs to reason and order. It accepts that all things in creation have rights, and that a universal righteousness depends upon a harmony that reconciles the rights of all things. This means that, while all creatures will have to give up some of their rights, none will have to give up all. Furthermore, the creature will be used in accord with its design; nothing will be done to pervert its purpose and function.

An example will show how early this notion came to the Hebrew mind. Deuteronomy 22:6,7 shows how a wild fowl can achieve its rights, while giving glory to God and satisfaction to man. If a Hebrew finds a nesting bird he must consider the Law in regard to rights. If he is hungry, he has a right to feed himself. Yet the mother has a right to her young, and the eggs have a right to be hatched. These are intrinsic rights. They can be reconciled only by the partial fulfilment of each right. It would be wrong to take the mother with her eggs. This would destroy the giver with the gift. Such a thing would be not only unethical, it would be an abomination. An equal evil would be to take the mother and leave the eggs. This would be a perversion of their purpose; the eggs could neither become fledglings, nor could they be used to feed others. A reconciliation of rights, therefore, would be for the passerby to take an egg or two, and to leave the rest for the mother. This would give respect to the creature and glory and thanks to God.

We have spoken here of perversion and abomination. This draws us from considerations of righteousness to those of holiness. To the Hebrew, it was more than unrighteous to use things in a way that was contrary to their design. It was confusion; it was perversion; it was abomination. This was a dangerous thing, for to pervert the purpose and function of a thing was to insult its Creator. It was to risk the possibility that He would be far more offended than He would be with a simple injustice. To get on the wrong side of God in this way was to get enmeshed in a new kind of evil—a more dangerous one, if only because of its irrationality. One could not remedy this kind of offense by the simple rules of justice. It got one into the complications of *taboo*, the nonrational but intensely personal matter that had to do with the hidden and often violent springs of identity.

Much of the Law can be seen as having to do with taboo, rather than with matters of ethics. The worst abomination would be the perversion of sex and order in the family and in the worshipping community. This accounts for the provisions of the Law against mingling different kinds of seed in a field, against eating unlike kinds of food, against wearing garments of diverse materials, yoking unlike animals in a team, and wearing clothes of the opposite sex. To obey these rules was to symbolize one's attention to the larger ethical values. The idea of abomination and taboo explains why not only murder and adultery were punishable by death, but also homosexuality, seduction, bestiality, cursing or striking one's parent, and blaspheming God. Each of these was an abomination—a perversion of function and order.

We cannot drop the matter of holiness at this point. It has a causal relation to righteousness in much the same way that faith is related to good works. The relation is well stated by G. K. Chesterton:

Morality did not begin by one man saying to another, "I will not hit you if you do not hit me"; there is no trace of such a transaction. There is a trace of men having said, "We must not hit each other in the holy place." They gained their morality by guarding their religion. They did not cultivate courage. They fought for the shrine and found they had become courageous. They did not cultivate cleanliness. They purified themselves for the altar, and found that they were clean. . . . The Ten Commandments which have been found substantially common to mankind were merely military commands; a code of regimental orders, issued to protect a certain ark across a certain desert. Anarchy was evil because it endangered the sanctity. And only when they had made a holy day for God did they find that they had made a holiday for men.[5]

Relation of Myths, Symbols, and Values

Perhaps the easiest way to see the relation between the absolutes of identity and value is to see how symbols relate to the myths that "precede" them and to the values that proceed from them. The elemental myth is that of creation. It holds that God made man from the dust of the earth, that He gave him a Law to follow, and punished him for disobeying that Law. This, of course, is no myth; it is very real indeed. The only mythical elements in the creation narrative are those that particularize and historicize the reality. Sin had to be traced back to its beginning, and the logical place to find it was in the first creature who had free will. The pretense of historicity was necessary to give a psychological validity to the symbol. The symbol that was encapsulated in the myth was this: man is created in the image of God. It had to follow that man has the potential of a personal relation with God. The myth describes the relation.

Before God ever made Himself known, man's experience of life had taught him all that he needed to know about function and design. Man's knowledge of relationship and value, his experience as a creator, had shown him the possibility of absolutes. His intuition pointed to the possibility of an absolute justice and an absolute love that were far above the relativities of human love and justice. Once God revealed Himself, and once He had appropriated, for the divine-human relation, the symbols that man was already familiar with, those symbols became absolutes in a new and vital setting. Therefore the Law that linked itself to those symbols was an absolute as well. It did not matter about the myths; those were only of man's devising. It was the symbols that were important—and the values that derived from them. God was a Father to those whom He adopted in a covenant relation: their due was one of obedience. God was a Savior to Israel: the people owed Him love.

The Law's potential for people today is suggested in a symbol God gave to Moses. When the people were about to enter the Promised Land this is the offer He made: if they would be faithful to Him the land would be faithful to them. The covenant was described in a metaphorical relation. Israel-the-people would be a bride to God, who would be a faithful husband to them. Israel-the-land would be a bride to Israel-the-people, who would go into her and possess and protect her. They would be her husbandmen, and she would provide her fruits of increase. The sense is that of an algebraic equation, $a:b::b:c$. The promise held that the faithfulness of the one was bound up with fidelity to the other.

Here is an insight into man's relation with God and nature at a time when modern technology, newly married to ancient greed, is poisoning man's environment and threatening an end to life on earth. The covenant gave identity and purpose to nature by clothing it with a semblance of personhood. It suggested that man's stewardship may best be fulfilled by treating the land as an equal. It suggests also that responsible stewardship not only does not treat *persons* as things; it does not even treat *things* as things.

Social Value of Tradition

In what has been said so far, it seems clear that the main purpose of the Law is neither *pro*scribing nor *pre*scribing what man will do, but in *de*scribing what he will be. The Law's purpose is much the same as that of tradition—

transferring what is identifying from one generation to another. The iconoclast objects to tradition on the ground that it preserves ignorance and prejudice through the sanctification of myth and symbol. At its best, tradition is the antithesis of this. It conserves and transmits social personality in the only possible manner.

It is not surprising that situationists should reject as null the wisdom of earlier generations; this is a compulsive trait of random-direction. What is surprising is that, at a time when the subconscious mind dominates man's thoughts of self as never before, the symbols that underlie his values and identity should be allowed to disintegrate. This has happened because man is preoccupied with his situation, rather than with his symbols and values. The need for concern with the latter—which is what tradition is—has been well expressed by Chesterton:

> Tradition may be defined as an extension of the franchise. Tradition means giving votes to the most obscure of all classes, our ancestors. It is the democracy of the dead. Tradition refuses to submit to the small and arrogant oligarchy of those who merely happen to be walking around. All democrats object to men being disqualified by the accident of birth; tradition objects to their being disqualified by the accident of death.[6]

In discussing tradition, we are getting away from absolutes like the Law. Tradition has an essential function, but it is not an absolute in itself. It *can* point to the false and harmful. But it also can point to what is real and true. The absolutes that tradition conveys are the same that the Law describes. They are concerned even more with social than with individual character. This is what makes them offensive to other- and to random-directed persons. Having a weak sense of social identity, they cannot be convinced that there *is* any such thing. Hence their determination to rid the world of the ancient superstitions of myth and symbol.

While tradition is not in itself an absolute, it is an absolute need in society. It transmits what has been divinely revealed, and what *may* be revealed only once. Any revelation of God—whether of His person or of the symbols and values that give identity to men—can only by tradition be carried to the men who were not there. Furthermore, the absolute has to be conveyed in earthen vessels, such as the Bible and the Church. These vessels, however frail they may be in themselves, are holy because they are the bearers of the holy.

Value of Absolutizing the Law

There is an important reason why an absolute such as the Law must touch the individual as well as his society. Society is transformed only by the transformation of individuals. The processes of salvation act only upon the individual. In the eternal setting, man's social character is primarily a means of helping individuals develop selves in this life. From this perspective, we can see why every individual must ultimately discover that the Law is the only pattern for man. The reasons why the Law has to be a given are now apparent. First, the Law is the only objective yardstick that man can measure himself by. It is the absolute that men are always looking for, and cannot often see in the behavior of those around them. Second, the Law is a signpost pointing to God. It is an absolute set in the midst of a world of uncertainties, directing man's attention to an absolute Lawgiver. The third reason for the Law's givenness is eschatological. The Law is a means by which man can judge his Maker as well as himself. Men who accept the Law in faith are able to judge themselves willingly and without being destroyed by guilt. They begin, thereby, to grow up in the Law's pattern. On the other hand, men who reject the Law are unwittingly judging God as well as themselves. In denying the essential pattern of their own manhood, they limit the possibility of relations with God. They cease, in an ever increasing degree, to be men.

Moral laws differ in a significant way from creation's other laws. As is also true with spiritual laws, they cannot be proven to the satisfaction of those who choose not to believe in them. Scientific laws, by contrast, can be proven to the satisfaction of all who can use their minds. The reason is that these laws' results are predictable and prompt. There is little time lag between cause and effect. Because of this, belief in scientific law is only a matter of intelligence; it has nothing to do with character. One does not become a better person by believing in a law of physics. It does not increase one's virtue by trying to obey it. A moral law, by contrast, must be obeyed before it can transform character, and it must be believed before it can be proven. Yet if it is not obeyed, it does not matter whether it is believed or not. The punishment is the same for those who accept it and for those who do not. The difference is that the man who does not believe in the Law does not even realize that he is being punished. He sees no moral cause and effect. He can see, perhaps, the connection between his adultery and his divorce. But he cannot see why his sinful act—and even more, why his sinful state of mind—should affect the identity of his wife, his children, and himself.

Two other things can be said about the Law as an absolute. One is that, just as with the laws of nature, violations bring automatic punishment. Except for those who detect and judge their own infractions—and who can be healed by divine forgiveness—there is no escape. Mostly the punishment is a punishment of *being*, and is as secret as the crime. The hater, for example, becomes a hateful man. But the punishment is sure, and it seems to fit the crime. In this the Law differs from human statutes. Even though a statute is called "law," a violator is never punished unless he is caught. If neither he nor anyone else is aware that an offense has been committed, it is not likely that there *is* an offense. No one is aware of one, and it is possible that no one has been hurt. The reason punishment cannot be automatic in the violation of a statute is that statutes are not really law, but only *types* of Law. They refer more to myth than they do to reality. And even when upheld by a Supreme Court, they are not necessarily just. They are signs that point to the chief idolatry—that man, not God, is god.

The other thing pertains to the *hiddenness* of the Law.

We have noted that the Law is sure, and that punishment for its violation is certain. We have also seen that even intelligent men must be able to reject the Law for seemingly honest reasons. The hiddenness of the Law is required in an absolute sense for men to have any freedom. The Law must be quite as hidden to those who choose not to see it as is the God who gave it. Jesus hinted at this need both for hiddenness and freedom when He told His disciples why He taught the multitude in parables, "that seeing they might *not* see, and hearing they *might* not understand."*
If the Law is to achieve its purpose in those who choose to believe in it, all men must be free to reject it for reasons that are satisfactory to them. Its truth cannot be as obvious as is that of the arithmetic table. Belief in the Law, like belief in God, requires the dismissal of doubts in order for faith and obedience to make a contribution to character.

The Jews' Unique Social Identity

One quality in Jewish identity has always been unique. It is the ability to combine individuality and corporality. Because of this, Jewish identity has changed little since the time of Ezekiel. Corporality and individuality are not found in separate cultures, as they are in the gentile world. They are one in the Jew, partly because of a unique trait and partly because of a unique understanding of God. The Jew, unlike the gentile, is able to live with paradox. For him, individual identity and membership in a body are both of the greatest importance. This is why Judaism, of all the world's cultures, has never had a rise and fall. The Jew has retained his twin sense of identity because he can be comfortable with paradox, and because he has kept his traditions. He has accepted the advantages of unrelated associations without being confused by the multiple faiths around him. Consequently, he has never taken the idea of universalism seriously.

Christianity contends that there is a later and higher revelation of God than the one He gave the Jews. Yet in

*Luke 8:10 (AV; italics mine)

spite of this, Christian identity has not generally measured up to that of the Jews. Having been adopted as spiritual children of Jacob, they are still the natural sons of Esau. We can appreciate this if we think of Jacob and Esau as progenitors, respectively, of Jew and gentile races. Esau was the more sympathetic character. He was manly, and his father's favorite. Jacob was a "mother's boy" and a cheat. Yet Jacob had qualities of greatness that his brother lacked utterly, and it was this that distinguished the one's descendants from the other's. Jacob's very lust for life was what led him to do wrong. In grasping at his brother's birthright and blessing, he showed how he valued the good. Esau did not really identify himself with these things at all. He did not deeply care. He was not faithful to God or to his unborn seed. Esau married strange women, and worshipped strange gods. As a result, he begot strange children who, within a generation or two, had lost their social identity. Jacob, by contrast, labored fourteen years to get a wife who could bear children with the character he desired. The living presence of his seed—a people whose social identity has been unchanging for more than a hundred generations—is witness to Jacob's faithfulness to God, to himself, and to his children.

Nevertheless, if the Jews have been faithful to God in being themselves, they have not been faithful to His larger purposes. They never became "a light to lighten the gentiles."* Both Jews and Christians have failed to bring mankind into a unity of fellowship under God. The Christians, because they are gentiles, are able to identify with the "other"; but they cannot long remain themselves. With the Jews it is the reverse. They have maintained themselves admirably, but they cannot identify with an "other." Of equal importance, they are unable to get the "other" to identify with them.

Part of the reason the Jews have remained themselves is that they have kept an unchanging tradition. In so doing, of course, they have lost a great many of their own into the gentile world. These have given up the tradition of their fathers, and have simply disappeared. The cost of

*Luke 2:32 (AV)

remaining themselves has been that the Jews have lost out in relative numbers. In the two thousand years of the Christian era the gentile population has expanded enormously. The Jews have stayed roughly the same. There were about ten million Jews in Jesus' time—the same number as today. During these centuries the Church itself has had a remarkable growth. It has transformed the world as has no other institution in history. Even so, there is always a danger of dissolution. Christians continue to be gentiles; they were never more so than they are right now. They are in constant danger of overidentifying with what they have been sent to transform.

A Pattern for Christian Identity

There is an identity-saving synthesis that Christians are able to claim. It is one that includes the Jews' trait of combining individuality and corporality. At the same time it leaves Christians open to the "other," so that they may fulfil their mission. As I shall show in the chapters ahead, this synthesis has always been a given in the Law of Christian Identity. Not only that, it has been tried and it has worked. It saved the Church in the declining years of Rome, and it brought Christian identity unscathed through the Dark Ages. It is something that offers promise for the future of man.

Since we have given a great deal of attention to four forms of social identity that are essentially secular, it is important that we should consider the possibility that there are religious forms of social identity. If there are any, they may be relevant to the secular forms and to the solution of their crisis. Especially will this be so if they can suggest a way in which the secular identity can be stabilized and maintained. This possibility exposes us to an idea that we have not yet considered, namely, that the best kind of social character combines the qualities of corporality, individuality, and "identification with the other." To achieve this would not necessarily require that men be exposed to the weaknesses of collective identity. It *might* mean that personal corporality and personal individuality could be unfolded for all men of good will. These could become universal traits because they were seen to be part of a single mold that is common to the race of men.

While this view is not far removed from the universalism that collectivists seek, it is utterly unsecular. It is, in fact, one thing that the collectivists could never achieve for themselves. They would necessarily fail because it is based upon an intrinsic description of man. This is the very ideal to which Jews and Christians have always looked. It looks to the reign of the Kingdom, and to the universal acceptance of the Fatherhood of God and the brotherhood of man. It envisions the joining together of the Old and the New Israel in one corporate body.

In the remaining chapters I shall try to show that such a view of identity is sufficient to stabilize a society that is already engulfed in the weakest phase of the secular cycle. It is a view of identity that I believe can meet man's needs, although there is little to suggest that it will be adopted.

A tragic thing has happened as a result of the schisms that rent the Church. The synthesis that bound Christian identity in the first millennium of the Church's history no longer exists. It therefore is no longer able to save. The synthesis dissolved because the Church itself came to a parting of the ways. In the millennium of schism a Church that had been one Church became three churches. One emphasized corporality, one emphasized individuality, and one emphasized "concern for the other." As these churches' influence varied from time to time, a cycle was set up that is not unlike the secular cycle I have described.

A particular danger for the West today is that the secular and the religious cycles are currently in phase. Instead of damping one another by reason of temporarily opposing forces, they are augmenting one another, and in so doing are exaggerating the effects that singly would not be so strong. Each of the cycles is in a phase that emphasizes "concern for the other" at the expense both of individuality and of the corporate heart of life. Here is one reason why the Church, which normally is the cement of the social fabric, is regarded by some people as a force for social dissolution. While this cannot long be true, the forsaking of tradition by those who are supposed to be its guardians has undoubtedly contributed to the identity crisis in the West. The resulting agony makes it possible for a poet like William Butler Yeats to exclaim, "Things fall apart; the center cannot hold;/ Mere anarchy is loosed upon the world."[7]

I shall try to show that there is a Christian *and* Jewish concept of identity that is intrinsic in man because it has originated in the mind of God. It is not explicitly revealed, but it seems to be there nonetheless. If this is so, the knowledge of that form of identity can bring renewal of life and hope to a world that is in despair. Especially is this so if along with that knowledge there is a way to apply it. Having this, men of faith can ever be hopeful about the future. Their own social identity can be maintained even in the midst of a universal decay. At the very least they can hold out, as Jews and Christians did in the Dark Ages— islands of personhood in a weltering sea of barbarism. At the best, the West itself may recapture its vanishing sense of identity. In any case, men of God need expose themselves to no further degradation. Knowing themselves and trusting in Him, they may continue to be recipients of His grace.

The cycle of identity that I have described thus far—the one that terminates in a weak and impersonal collectivism—offers no hope at all to the world. Nevertheless, it does not have to be. What I shall try to demonstrate is that, while it is in itself an inexorable cycle, its continuance is by no means inevitable.

Notes on Chapter Six:

1. Jean-Paul Sartre, *Existentialism* (New York: Philosophical Library, 1947), p. 33.
2. Paul Tillich, *Love, Power and Justice* (London: Oxford University Press, 1954), p. 4.
3. Sir Walter Moberly, *Responsibility* (Greenwich, Ct.: Seabury Press, 1956), p. 59.
4. Paul Tillich, *Love, Power and Justice*, p. 76.
5. G. K. Chesterton, *Orthodoxy* (Garden City, N.Y.: Doubleday, 1959), p. 68.
6. *Ibid.*, p. 48.
7. William Butler Yeats, *The Second Coming.*

Chapter Seven

PERSONAL PATTERNS
IN THE GODHEAD

This book's concern is not the personhood of God. It is the personhood of man. I am not aiming for conversions, but for the recovery of social character. Yet, because we are concerned for what is intrinsic to the life of man, we must at this point refer to One who is said to have created the forms that exist in man. We must study the structure of personhood in a God who is supposed to have revealed all that man needs to know for a fruitful relationship with Him. If God *is*, and if He has indeed fashioned us in His image, we can be sure that what He has told us about Himself can tell us a lot about ourselves.

I am well aware that in any such study our thinking may be unrealistic because of our anthropomorphism. We may be merely projecting our thought patterns and our identity patterns in a Godward direction. But we have already learned that we do not go astray by anthropomorphizing in the other direction. We have found that there is safety in thinking that when a dog wags his tail his intentions are peaceable, and that when he growls and bares his teeth his intentions are aggressive. We need not be afraid to run an intellectual risk. There is a great deal of evidence to suggest that when we impute personhood to God we are, in fact, engaging in a two-way projection.

Christians must be the first to admit the possibility of anthropomorphism when they speak of God as their Father. For one thing, they cannot think of Him as their

141

begetter. Their relationship with Him is that of adopted children. To them God is a Creator—a creator of man and of fatherhood itself. Yet because Jesus teaches them to think of God as their Father as well as His, and because He instituted a rite that makes them children by adoption, they can now speak of the Father in terms that may be real. After all, they did not make up the idea of the Fatherhood of God, or of the brotherhood of those who are incorporated into Christ. These are objectively given concepts.

So we begin by looking for personal patterns that seem to be implicit in the Godhead. We shall try to see if there is any connection between the patterns we have seen in ourselves and the patterns we find in God. If we can see a similarity, we can assume one of two things. Either the symbols of Judeo-Christian identity are sure and certain, or we have an enormous debt to some old but fallacious assumptions.

There are a number of patterns of identity and character that we can find in the Godhead. Some are patterns that we can identify with because they are also descriptive of us. For example, God is personal, just, and loving. So, to a degree, are we. Other traits of God are so untypical of us that they identify God all the more clearly as Himself. He is eternal, infinite, all-knowing, almighty. We are none of these things. We never can or shall be.

The patterns to which I shall draw attention are those that refer to social identity, and that are common both to God and man. These will show that man, as a social being, has a resemblance to God. They are summed up in seven propositions, of which this chapter will be an elucidation. Each of these propositions is offered as an axiom; that is, it seems to demand acceptance as a given. While this may seem to be a piece of arrogance, I believe that none of the axioms is contrary to the nature God has revealed. All are rooted in the Christian doctrine of the Trinity.

The first axiom comes straight out of the Book of Genesis:

Because he is created in the image of God, man is essentially personal.

This proposition is, by its very nature, the elemental one in any study of man. It refers to man's freedom, accountability, and "id entity." If one rejects the image symbol on the ground that it is supported only by myth, it must be asserted that nothing but biblical religion can successfully posit personhood in either God or man. Personhood is the most indefinable characteristic of man because it is the most unfathomable mystery in the Godhead. The creation myth adds all to the symbol that any story can. It gives an intuitive answer to the *why* question. This is the question that science, which is limited to giving answers to *what* and *how*, can never give a clue to. It says that man is like his Creator, and it explains why this is so.

The second axiom is this:

The attainment of personhood in man lies in identification with God.

The creation narrative is not as gentle with man as is the doctrine of behaviorism. It does not let him off the hook because the inconsistency of his nature allows him to give in to temptation. It holds that man is alienated from his essential self not because of the will of God, but because of his own misuse of freedom.

It was not until man had experienced a loss of self that he had to be given a Law. Even then, man did not see himself in the Law. It took the grace of God for man to perceive that the Law was his very pattern—the measure of his being. The Gospel, when it came, conveyed a higher insight. *The Gospel declared that it is not the Law, so much as God Himself, that is the true Pattern of man.* Because this is so, man's wholeness may be restored by a personal engagement with God.

Man requires religion. More than that, he requires a God-given religion. This is so because, within the limitations of his nature, *man is absolutely free and responsible—*

yet absolutely dependent upon God. It is the paradoxical fact of freedom and dependence that makes the relationship necessary.

We cannot overlook that human personhood, if it is to progress beyond the barest minimum, requires a *revealed* religion. The religion must be a given, and the circumstances of man's encounter with God must be those of God's choosing, not man's. Before there can be any mutual knowledge, the Hidden must choose to disclose Himself. Without self-disclosure, God can only be assumed in conjecture, projection, phantasy. None of these is real. They are only make-believe.

There are three religions that can be called revealed—religions that point to God as one and personal. They are Judaism, Christianity, and Islam. For our purposes there are only two. Islam, while it is historically the latest, is the most primitive in terms of revelation. It is the least adequate so far as man's identity is concerned. Islam has something to say about personhood, but Judaism and Christianity say it better. Islam is not a progressive religion; that is to say, its revelation does not tell something about God that had not been known before. What God told Muhammad about Himself, He had long before revealed to Abraham.

Islam is the religion of Abraham, without being the religion of Moses or of Christ. Islam's devotee has to settle for something less than full personality because his God is not willing to share his personhood. The austere and lonely God of Muhammad is one of blazing, blinding personality. He is total Will—and he does not share any part of that trait. His plan for history is a predestinating Fate. Man therefore has no freedom. As a result, man is something less than divine. He is, in fact, a good deal less than what Jewish and Christian tradition holds man was meant to be.

Principles of Personality Formation

Now that we have seen the possibility of an identity pattern that God projects upon man, let us reflect upon some principles of personality formation. There are three that I should like to offer, all relating to identification with others—whether those others be man or God.

    a. We tend to become like those persons whom we most admire.

    b. We tend to become what we believe about them.

    c. We tend to become what we do in relation to them, whether in their presence or in their absence.

These propositions need little explaining. Of the three, the first is the key one, since it explains *why* identification takes place. The second and third explain *how* identification takes place: the way we identify. The things we believe and do about those we admire are the process of our becoming.

This process, of course, requires a relationship of trust and love. Those whose identification with God is one of boredom or suspicion are apt to grow worse—not better. This suggests a fourth proposition that is a corollary of the first:

    d. We tend to be shaped adversely by those to whom we are hostile.

It is not uncommon for people who have been reared in the Church to have been done a great deal of harm. They become not the restored image, but the more greatly defaced image, of God. They acquire traits that are the inverse of those God projects. This is something that many psychiatrists have noted. It cannot point to any fault in God, but it can and does point to a defect in what people have believed about God, and in the example they have shown.

This is enough to stress the importance of identifying with the God who really is. The first principle is the most important. We identify with God because He is our God and we are His children. The second and third principles are the ones that point up the process. They touch upon what is "formal" in religion. *What we believe* relates to the forms of religious *faith*. *What we do* touches the forms of religious *practice*.

    The third axiom is:

Man's basic form, like that of God, is trinity in unity.

One of the most primitive ideas of the Hebrews—shared with other childlike people—is that the things a man owns partake of his personality. There is a lively intuition in this. The things that are identified with us *do* tend to describe us. A cabinetmaker's work, for example, points to the skill, the patience, and the attention to details that reside in the man himself.

There is a difference between the thing made and the child begotten, however, and here we must part company with the primitive mode of thought. The thing can only manifest the maker's character. The child can be a partaker of his personhood. Not only will the child be similar as an individual; he will be one with the father in a corporate identity. Upon this observation shall be based our references to the similarities that we find in God and man and nature. The trinities that we find in nature and man may show the *form* of God; but it is in the qualities that occur in man's character that we find a clue to the *nature* of God.

There are an astonishing number of trinities that occur in man as well as in nature. They certainly hint at, if they do not prove, the threefold form of God. There is trinity in matter; it consists of solids, liquid, and gas. There is trinity in space—length, breadth, and height. There is trinity in time—past, present and future. There is a trinity of forms in skeletal animals—beasts and fish and birds.

When we come to the trinities of man's life we approach the essential trinities of God. This is not only because man shares God's character, but also because he shares His personhood. Each of the trinities in man relates to the dynamics of identity. In himself, man is a trinity of body, mind, and spirit. His apprehension of the absolute touches a trinity of beauty, truth, and goodness. His life as a moral person requires the interaction of justice, love, and power. His concern with social personality requires the continual definition of freedom, responsibility, and obedience.

Are all these trinities real, or is it only our human psychology that makes us see things in threes? Possibly both. It is significant that the symbolic thought both of Judaism and Christianity is full of reference to trinity. Whatever their belief about God, the psychology of each is trinitarian. Perhaps this is why the Jew equals the Christian in freedom, responsibility, and obedience.

Christianity is the only religion that is wedded to a tripersonal God. Considering the trinities in human psychology, a triune God may seem to be only an anthropomorphic projection. Nevertheless, the Christian *doctrine* is not psychological. It is based upon a given—the teachings of Jesus, the recollections of the Gospel writers, and the experience of the early Church.

This brings us to the point that there is no real trinity unless there is also unity. God is not so much Trinity as He is triune. He is Three in One and One in Three. This is what the Christians claim for God. It is also true of creation. There is only one real time: past, present, and future are only a way of dividing it. There is only one real space. The same can be said for matter. Water can be liquid or ice or steam; no matter which, it is water. And so it is with man. Whether he be looked upon as a trichotomy of mind, will, and emotions or of body, mind, and spirit, he is still man and he is essentially one.

This argument does not apply to the form of God's personality, but it surely applies to His nature. God is not only Love or Justice or Power; He is all three in one. It is only when we come to the personhood of God that we come to the elemental form of trinity. God can be God without being Godhead; Allah is One and Yahweh is One. But there can be no Godhead without plurality in personality. When God says, "Let *us* make man in *our* image, after *our* likeness,"* He seems to be speaking as more than One.

In order to see why Christians regard Godhead as essential to Godhood, we must think of the dynamics of love. As John says, "God is love."† We know that God is eternal, which means that God has been love from the

*Gen. 1:26 (AV)
†1 John 4:8

beginning. But what does that involve? God cannot simply have loved Himself; this is the difficulty with a God like Muhammad's. The Christian would understand that it was out of the dynamic of love *within* the Godhead that God chose to create. It took a pre-existent love for God to be able to say, "Let us make man in our image." Love requires a trinity—a subject, an object, and an act of loving. The Father is the Lover, the Son is the Beloved, and the Spirit is the dynamic of Love. Yet these Three are One. The dynamic is endless and eternal. The Persons are each to each, co-acting, co-receiving, in each co-inhering. Within the Godhead is this interaction, ever seen and experienced in terms of personhood and function.

At this point we can see in the Godhead the patterns of social identity. God is individual Three in corporate One, with a loving concern for all He has made. In His revelation in Christ—giving a set of data that has been hammered into doctrine by the Church—we can detect the shape of what we have been studying all along. The terms we have used, in fact, provide the elements for a new definition of the Trinity. It is one that may be more satisfying to contemporary man than are the formularies of the past.

Since the fourth century, Christians have talked of God as being Three Persons in One Godhead. Although they have known the Godhead as personal, they have never said as much in any of their creeds. Instead of dealing with the mystery of triune personality, they have dealt with concepts like *ousia (substance)* and *hypostasis (essence)*. In resolving the Arian controversy, the Church decided that God had three *hypostaseis* and one *ousia*. The Nicene Creed declared God to be Three Persons who are One in substance. The intention of the Nicene Council was to guard against tritheism, and yet at the same time to avoid Docetism.* Because it had given no thought to the sociology of personality, it did not say what is being stated

---

*The docetists were a gnostic sect who, from the first century onward, had contended that God was but one Person, of whom Christ had been a temporary manifestation. They discounted the meaning of the Cross by asserting that Jesus only *appeared (dokein, to seem)* to be a person, and that he only *seemed* to suffer.

here—that *God is Three Persons in One Person.* In terms of
our present understanding, God is *He*, whether He be
Three or One. He is three separate and distinct Persons in
one corporate Godhead. Each has His own identity, His
own properties, and His own function in the economy that
extends into creation. Here in the Godhead we can see the
patterns for the personhood of man. We can see corporality and individuality. We can see concern for the other.

Here is the fourth axiom:

**Man's personhood is formed by the knowledge he has of
God—as immanent, transcendent, incarnate.**

There are only three ways in which man can know God
as He has revealed Himself. God is *immanent*, He is *transcendent*, and He is *incarnate*. These are the three most
significant *properties* of God, as contrasted with His *virtues.* Our knowledge of them is a part both of our intuition and of the biblical revelation. An understanding of
these properties is vital to personal identity. Because these
terms are not found in everyday use, we would do well to
consider their meaning. *Immanent*, put simply, means
here—not *there.* It means *in* and *all around.* An immanent
God is an indwelling God. Though unseen, He is never far
away. While He cannot be confused with creation itself, He
is *in* and *present to* His people. This does not mean that He
is universally and equally present; that is the pantheist's
mistake. The God who is immanent in creation is more
present to what is good than to evil. He is more identified
with what is personal than with what is not. It seems likely
that the spirit who is present to evil is none other than
Satan himself. Immanence would be the most strategic
posture of one whose kingdom is of this world, and who
desires to identify men with himself.

Christians understand the Immanent Spirit to be the
Holy Ghost. He is the one Person in the Godhead who is
always present to those who seek Him. He is "the Spirit of
God (who) moved upon the face of the waters,"* when He

*Gen. 1:2 (AV)

created the ancient world. He is the Spirit who overshadowed Mary in begetting the Holy Child.*

By contrast with immanent, *transcendent* means *out there*—not *here*. It connotes a God who is far away. Not only is such a God a distant God who dwells outside time and space. He is beyond all understanding. He is ineffable, unknowable, *mysterium tremendum*. He is all-holy, almighty, omniscient. Even in thinking about such a God, man has to be filled with reverence and awe.

It is not surprising that, in Jewish and Christian theology, the Transcendent God can be known only through a mediator whom He has chosen. Aside from the shadowy priest-king, Melchizedek, through whom Abraham gave sacrifices, Moses was the first of God's mediators. The mediatorial office is a necessity, both for knowledge of and relationship with the Transcendent One of heaven. This is the testimony of Abraham, Moses, the Prophets, Muhammad. Finally, it is the testimony of Christ, who said, "No man cometh to the Father but by me."† Transcendence, in the Christ-revealed Godhead, is the property of God the Father.

An incarnate God is one who has revealed Himself by becoming something other than spirit. He has made Himself known by other channels than the supernatural. *Incarnate* means *enfleshed.* In its divine sense, it means that God has entered history by becoming a man. In Jesus Christ, the transcendent and immanent God has extended Himself into the dimensions of our manhood. He has done this so that man can know Him more truly, and so that man can enter a more fulfilling relationship with Him.

Aside from this ultimate act, there is an incarnational principle. It holds that God sanctifies some forms of the particular in order to enable man to join Him in effecting His universal purposes. God permits certain times, places, things, events, people, and ceremonies to be identified with His holiness. He uses particular *channels* for His grace; using them, men are more easily able to identify with Him.

*Luke 1:35
†John 14:6 (AV)

God also blesses a particular people, so that they, acting in cooperation with Him, can bring a blessing upon the whole race of men.

Incarnational religion is one that men apprehend even before they are aware of immanence or transcendence. It is psychologically a necessity; this in itself points to the possibility of its being objectively true. For Christians, Christ is the Messiah whose coming was foretold by the Prophets. He is the Torah who was made known to Moses. He is the Logos who was intuited by the Jews of the Dispersion. There is incarnationalism in other religions besides Judaism and Christianity, however. All had an intuition of Christ, and of incarnate personhood in God. These include the primitive animisms that impute personhood to rocks and hills and streams. They include the psychological religions of the East, which have a high sense of ethic, and which have discovered some of the secrets of personality. They include Islam, which is as purely transcendental as a religion can be. Even Islam has to use the sacramental principle. Allah has revealed himself in one particular prophet. His revelation is presently confined to one particular book. He has sanctified certain seasons and some particular cities. In Mecca there is one particularly holy shrine. These are the necessary ways in which the universal God, to meet the psychological needs of men, has revealed and enshrined Himself.

Even God's trinity was intuited before it was revealed. Psychological religion is very ancient; man thought of God from the beginning as the measure of himself. Perhaps the first apprehension of the Spirit was the thought of a hovering, immanent mother. The gods of the primitive agriculturalists combined the life-giving and sustaining properties of the Spirit with a sacramentalizing of growth. For them, mother earth became an Earth Mother.

Likewise, transcendence was first intuited by dwellers in the desert, and by those who ventured the seas. For them, reality lay in the heavens rather than in the earth. They would have understood the divine transcendence as that of a father who was immanent only at the moment of conception, and who had thenceforth lived at a distance.

As for the divinely incarnate, it is not surprising that virtually every primitive religion had a myth of a virgin birth and of a "coming one." These showed the real understanding that the only ultimate mediator must be a Person who is both God and man. In his intuition of the Messiah, primitive man was unwittingly worshipping the Incarnating God in whom the Virgin Birth would one day become a reality.

Even as the properties of the Persons of the Godhead differ, so also do their functions. It is more than mere anthropomorphism that those functions that are imputed to the Godhead complement themselves in trinity. To a large degree, it is a matter of biblical revelation. For example, John describes Christ as the Word of God. In a trinity of *personal activity*, God the Son is the *Mind* or *Logos*. The Holy Spirit is the pattern for *Affections* or feelings. The Father is the pattern for *Will*. The projection fits both revelation and intuition. It is quite proper to ascribe will, which is the central function in personality, to the One whom both Bible and Church hold to be the First Person of the Godhead.

Likewise, in a trinity of moral activity, the Father must be regarded as the pattern for justice, the Son as the pattern for love, and the Spirit as the pattern for power. The three are qualities that complement and fulfil one another; they can be raised up to an absolute only in the Godhead.

In the same way, the Godhead is the matrix for a trinity that is essential to human *becoming*. This is the trinity of freedom, responsibility, and obedience. The Father is the prototype of responsibility, the Son is that of obedience, and the Spirit is that of freedom. This is not mere invention. The Father is the source of law and order: this is the message of Sinai. The Spirit identifies Himself with evolution and change, and He is the One to whom Jesus referred when He said,

> The *pneuma* (wind) bloweth where it listeth, and thou hearest the sound thereof, but canst not tell whence it cometh and

whither it goeth: so is everyone that is born of the *Pneuma* (Spirit).*

As to the Son, Christians look upon Him as showing absolute perfection in all three of these virtues. But chiefly He made Himself known in being obedient unto death.

Trinities in Judaism

Judaism and Christianity have a similar apprehension, not only of God's form, but also of his personality. For Christians, the Father is one and the same with El Shaddai, who revealed Himself to Abraham. He is the Transcendent Person who is also the God of Muhammad. The God that Moses spoke of was a striking contrast with the God of Abraham. Yahweh was not only transcendent; He was immanent as well. His transcendence was hid in a pillar of cloud. His immanence was revealed in the pillar of fire. Instead of being only a predestinarian God who stood outside human history, Yahweh was also a providential God who acted in history—even to the extent of seeming to overrule Himself. He took His people out of slavery. He led them through many perils with a mighty, outstretched arm. Not only did Yahweh save His people then; He also saves them now. Because Jews know God as both transcendent and immanent, they are able to identify with Him in both dimensions, and so to acquire His virtues. Christians see the properties that Yahweh revealed to Moses as being those of the Holy Spirit.

It is true that the Jews had no knowledge of an Incarnate Son. Among the religions of antiquity, theirs was alone in having only the vaguest notion of a virgin birth, an atoning death, and a resurrection. Jesus was the first Jew to find these things in the Scriptures, and to perceive that the incarnational principle pointed to a personal reality. Now that the pattern has been fulfilled, Christians can easily trace it in the Scriptures. The Jews cannot, and yet

*John 3:8 (AV)

they are greatly influenced by the pattern. They have the most remarkable social identity found in the history of man.

Here is a brief summary of the trinities that seem to be inherent in the Godhead, and to be projected from God to man.

Trinities of Property and Character Ascribed
Both to God and to Man

Having reference to God's	*Transcendence*	*Incarnation*	*Immanence*
Revelation in Judaism	El Shaddai	Torah, Logos	Yahweh
Person in Christian Trinity	Father	Son	Holy Spirit
Functions in personal choice	Will	Mind	Affections
Functions in moral choice	Justice	Love	Power
Functions in relationship	Lover	Beloved	Dynamic of Love
Character projected to man	Responsibility	Obedience	Freedom

Now let us see how these views of God have affected the Christian Church. In the years since 1054, when the Eastern and Western churches separated, the Church in the West has continued to split. Broadly speaking, it has become three separate churches, each oriented to one Person of the Trinity. Two give lip service to God as Triune. Only one is unitarian. Yet all have fallen short in the identity they have imparted to their members, because each has stressed one Person of the Godhead at the expense of the other two. Even where they have acknowledged God's tri-unity, they have neglected two of His properties (by which I mean God's transcendence, His immanence, and His incarnation). In failing to deal adequately with the Godhead, they have impeded the personal growth of their members.

Trinities in Christian Faith and Practice

Before describing these churches and the kind of men they have produced, let me mention several other trinities that govern Christians in their religious faith and practice.

The first is a trinity of modes of communication. It is one of thought, word, and deed. Thought takes care of communication with an immanent God. He is within, and closer than any mortal. Because of this, it is not necessary to pray aloud, or even to use words. Personal interaction with such a God moves directly from heart to heart. Because words are unnecessary, His worship is largely that of intuition and feelings. It is a worship that is formless and free. This is the mode of communication with God the Holy Spirit.

Communication with a transcendent God must take place in words. A deity at a distance cannot be approached by thought. He must be addressed aloud and formally. Not much ceremony is required, however; words are the important thing. In worshipping God the Father, men will not be concerned about how they look. Their chief concern will be whether they can be heard.

By contrast, communication with the Incarnate One can be done in word and deed. He is an Other, but He is sometimes close at hand. Men can rejoice to be in His presence. They can be elaborate in their ceremony because He is a King who has come for a visit. At such times He is *here*—not *there*. Because His worship is worship-in-deed, it can be as expressive as men choose to make it.

A second trinity is one of sources of divine authority. Each is called holy because it is given by God Himself. The three are: Holy Bible, Holy Church, and Holy Reason. They are the means by which God gives His revelation and keeps it fresh for every generation. Holy Bible is the Word of God; it relates chiefly to God the Father. Holy Church is the Deed of God, and belongs to God the Son. Holy Reason is the Thought of God. We associate it chiefly with God the Holy Spirit.

These three are not infallible. While *of* God, they are

not themselves God. They are channels that convey to man what is otherwise hidden. The Bible is, by its very nature, the least corruptible. Its holiness is limited only by the degree to which its writers were inspired, and by the accuracy with which their writings have been preserved and translated. The Church is more corruptible than the Bible, as any historian knows. Reason is the most corruptible of all.

A third trinity is that of forms of worship. In all the Church's history, only three have developed. Considering that there are three Persons in the Godhead, it is likely that there *can* be only three. Each seems to have been given by the Person in the Godhead with whom it is chiefly associated. The three forms of worship are the Holy Office, the Holy Eucharist, and the Holy Devotion, or prayer-meeting.

In its present form, the Office is the oldest of the three. It is a Bible-centered liturgy. It speaks to man with readings from the Scriptures. It speaks to God with psalms and prayers that are largely taken from the Scriptures. The Office is "formal" in that it has an intrinsic form, but it is a very simple service. Both in symbol and reality it is the worship of a deity-at-a-distance. Its communication is that of worship-in-word. It attends to the Transcendent Father.

The second form of worship is the Eucharist. It is given by God the Son. Although it has the form of a sacrifice offered to the Father—patterned in part after the Temple sacrifices—it culminates in an act of sacramental union between the Bride of Christ and her Lord. It is therefore chiefly an act that is oriented to Him. It is a formal and elaborate worship-in-deed, befitting the Son whose presence is celebrated.

The third mode of worship is the formless and quiet Devotion. It is derived from the expectant hush of Pentecost, when time seemed to stand still as men waited for the Descent of the Spirit. What kind of worship this *leads* to, of course, is without any limits or bounds. It may be prophetic utterance or a speaking in tongues. It may be an outpouring of evangelical fervor. It may simply be the continuance of a mystical identifying-with-God. Whatever it is, it cannot be bounded by rules or form. It is an utterly free worship in and of the Spirit.

As to the origins of these forms, the Eucharist is really the oldest. Whether as a thank-offering or a sin-offering, it originated in the sacrifices required by the Law of Moses. These came at a time when God was no longer thought of as only a predestinator, but also as divinely provident. They belong to a time when man dared approach God through a priest, instead of being limited to hearing from Him through a prophet.

The Office is derived from the sixth century B.C., when the Jews were carried into Exile. Being torn from the Temple, they were unable to make the offerings that their priesthood called for. The Office substituted word for deed; priest was replaced by rabbi. After the return from Babylon, the Jews continued to say the sacred Office. They did this even though the priesthood and the sacrifices had been restored. An advantage of the office was that it did not have to be said in the Temple. It took formal religion into countless villages and towns. It substituted synagogue for Temple, and family for tribe. When the Christians adopted the Office they took it into the monasteries, where it remained almost exclusively until the sixteenth century.

The Devotion, although unanticipated, was given by the Holy Spirit. It came, of course, at Pentecost. This event was more than a commissioning of the Church. It was a driving forth of the Church—filled with concern for others. It gave something to the New Israel that the Jews had never had before: the will and the way to proclaim God's Person and purposes to the gentiles.

Effects of Schism on Social Character

These, then, are the trinities that influence human *becoming:* the forms of communication and worship, and the sources of divine authority. Now that we are acquainted with them, we can see how it happened that the Church split in the way that it did. The three forms that the Church took were the Catholic, the Protestant, and the

Pentecostal. The Catholic church was oriented chiefly to the Son, the Protestant to the Father, and the Pentecostal to the Spirit.*

Even though it was trinitarian, Catholic Christianity could not help giving an unwitting emphasis to the Son, at the expense of the Father and the Spirit. It could not help emphasizing obedience at the expense of responsibility and freedom. Rome gave its people the worship-form of the Eucharist and the authority-source of the Church. The Office and the Devotion were never made available to the lay people, and the Bible and the Inner Light were actually suppressed.

The Protestants, by contrast, used the Bible as their authority-source, and the Office as their form of worship. They rarely used the Eucharist or the Devotion. They discounted the possibility of authority either in the Church or in Holy Reason. Because of this, there was a great difference in the men they produced. The Catholics, emphasizing the filial virtue of obedience, tended to produce followers. They stressed the importance of family and Church, and in so doing produced not a few saints. The Protestants, stressing the fatherly virtue of responsibility, tended to produce leaders.

The Pentecostalists, using the prayer-meeting and waiting for the Inner Light, obtained a still different result. Instead of emphasizing responsibility or obedience, they emphasized individual freedom. And they got it. They produced men who showed a capacity not only for meeting change, but for actually bringing it about. In stressing the reason-that-sets-men-free, they developed a genius for innovation, along with a talent for identification-with-others.

At the same time, the Spirit-oriented sects did not confess a triune God. Being oriented to the divine immanence, they felt no need for transcendence or incarnation. They had no trouble with communication, for the God they knew was within. Finding no need for a Mediator,

*Since the last two are both Protestant, it is easier to equate Father-orientation with the old-line *denominations*, and Spirit-orientation with the *sects*.

they wanted no priesthood or sacraments. They were not tied to tradition, as were the denominations. Yet they produced men who talked and acted like Christians.

Now we can see why the churches' forms of belief and practice have had such a profound effect. We can see why they touch not only individual character, but social identity as well. Catholic Christianity shows corporate identity because its forms of belief and practice *produce* corporate identity. Holy Church, as an authority-source, can be equated with nothing but the Body of Christ. The Eucharist is equally corporate. It is a tribal offering, requiring an altar and a priesthood. It requires a congregation that will think of itself not as a collection of individuals, but as members of a body. The Eucharist is both an expression of corporality and the means by which it is formed. It clothes the worshipper with tribal identity, and with all the corporate virtues.

Similarly, the Office encourages individualism in the worshipper. It is more than an accident that the Office originated at the very time Jewish individualism was beginning to be felt. The nationalism that had begun in Solomon's time was given a more radical thrust when the people were carried off to Babylon. The Office confirmed and enlarged the individuality they had already begun to feel. The Scriptures confirmed this too. The new forms of worship and authority did not stress "togetherness" so much as they did separateness and distinctness. Office and Bible made it possible for men to worship as families or as individuals, rather than corporately at the Temple. All a man had to do, to worship this way, was to learn to read.

It is quite understandable that when, much later, the Reformation came about, its leaders abandoned the Mass and the hierarchical Church. They were trying to break with corporality. They wanted to confirm their individualism by adopting a form of belief and practice that would enhance it. They found their ideal source of authority in the Bible, which had already been translated into the vernacular, and which the invention of printing had made universal. They found their ideal form of worship in the Office, which they borrowed from the monasteries. These things made it possible for a Christian man to identify directly with God. He did not have to worship in a church; he could worship at home with his wife and children. When away from home, he could worship by himself. He no longer was aware of any urgent need to identify with a cult.

The Devotion and the Inner Light carried individualism to its logical extreme. It set the Christian free to be at one with outsiders in the world. At the Quaker meeting each was the equal of every other. There was no such thing as a *padre;* there were only brothers and sisters. The leader was the Spirit within, who often chose the humblest in which to express Himself. The member's significance was expressed in the courtesy of "thee" and "thou." This address was more than symbolic; the second person singular gave the ultimate in personal dignity. In the Quaker meeting the individual had such importance that nothing could be done without his consent. There was no tyranny of majority rule; everyone had to agree. For the Quakers, Holy Reason was not consensus; it was the Light that shines in the darkness. The people to whom this Light was given could be at home anywhere. They could relate to those outside the fold, treating them as brothers. They were not susceptible to an empathetic loss of identity. They could keep their other-orientation because they were at one with themselves.

Religious Cycle of Social Identity

Now we can trace the cycle that resulted from the split in the Christian Church. In some respects it was not a cycle at all. It had neither regularity nor predictability. It had, rather, the appearance of a pendulum whose swing was checked, from time to time, in one of three different positions. Each was the congealed position of one branch of the Western Church. The cycle was a sequence of actions and reactions that developed in response to three seemingly antithetical forms of identity—*all rooted in the Godhead.* It was the consequence of a sundered Church giving varying importance to the elements of immanence, transcendence, and incarnation.

The direct cause of the Reformation was the rise of individualism in the West. Early in the Renaissance, man's understanding of personhood changed from one of *involvement* to one of *detachment*. At that time the centripetal forces that are always found in the social group were overcome by the individualizing, centrifugal forces. The Reformation froze, in its own preferred position, the pendulum that in a schism-free Church might have continued to move. The Counter-Reformation was a reactionary adjustment to the Reformation. It renewed the divine sanction of corporality—freezing the pendulum in another position.

There was a third force at work in this period. It was a reformation that took place within Protestantism itself. During the century after the Reformation and the Counter-Reformation, a Spirit-oriented sectarianism took shape, which resulted in a church that, for want of a better term, I have called Pentecostal. Pentecostalism had an important social significance, in that it extended individualism to the lower classes, whereas prior to this, individualism belonged only to the upper and middle classes. (It was conferred by the state religions—Anglican, Calvinist, and Lutheran.) Pentecostal nonconformity extended the franchise to everyone who had the gift of faith. The downtrodden no longer had to be submissive, or satisfy themselves with obedience. Their religion had set them free.

The greatest schism in the Church was not the result of individualism, however, for it came long before Western individualism began. It came as a result of the difficulty men had in reconciling the properties of immanence, transcendence, and incarnation. At the beginning the Church had been oriented to all Three Persons of the Trinity, both in belief and in worship. During the first millennium, however, stresses built up that led to a parting of the ways. Both the Eastern and Western churches had always been properly attached to the Person of God the Son. However, the Eastern Church was more concerned with the Transcendent Father than it was with the Holy Spirit. It was a mystical, other-worldly Body that never felt the need to change. Even though it suffered more than the West from the invasions from the East, it had always been able to keep an unchanging identity.

The Western Church, by contrast, was practical, energetic, this-worldly. It was always conscious of itself as an institution. It had been more immanental than transcendental from the earliest years of its history; and its immanentism became virtually assured in the fourth century, when the capital of the Empire was transferred from Rome to Constantinople. Because of a vacuum of leadership, the Roman Church acquired an immense interest in temporal affairs.

When the Renaissance dawned—bringing individualism with it—the immanental stance continued. While Rome may not have been especially oriented to the *Person* of the Spirit, it was engrossed in those things that belong to the Spirit's economy: reason, power, Church-extension, encouraging men to invest their freedom in a larger obedience to Christ. Reason and freedom, it felt, belonged more to the Body than to the individual. And, because reason is subject to corruption, and because freedom easily turns into license, Rome's immanentism got it into trouble. It was a trouble that the break with the East had done nothing to forestall. The northern Europeans, who were least identified with Rome, and who had political and economic reasons for a break, did just that. They made the break, both with the Church and with the Empire. Their reaction against immanence led them to stress the transcendental in religion. Both the secular and the religious view of life turned them to the Transcendent Father, whose worship could secure their individualism. In time, the Pentecostalists reacted against transcendence and returned to immanentism. They turned from the institutional Church and State to the one Person in the Godhead whom it is impossible to institutionalize—the Holy Comforter. However, while their orientation was to the Person of the Spirit, it did not include a this-worldly theology; at least it did not stress the Spirit's attention to the Church. It continued to emphasize individualism, and stressed even more profoundly than before the release of Spirit-filled individuals into the world, charged with concern for others.

Here is a summation of the trinities that give shape to social character—and of their evident results:

Trinities That Shape Social Character

Referring to God the	Father	Son	Holy Spirit
As required by his	Transcendence	Incarnation	Immanence
Trinity of communication-forms	Word	Deed	Thought
Trinity of forms of worship	Office	Eucharist	Devotion
Trinity of authority-sources	Bible	Church	Reason
Resultant virtues in man	Responsibility	Obedience	Freedom
Types of individual produced	Leader	Saint	Innovator-humanitarian
Resultant social personality	Individualism	Corporality	Identification-with-others
Projection into social personality of properties in Godhead	Detachment	Involvement with members of Body	Involvement with those outside the Body

The fifth axiom is this:

In imputing personhood to God, all religions do so in one or more of these ways: transcendence, immanence, incarnation.

Space and subject matter do not allow any extended proof of this point. However, it is largely self-evident. Transcendence, immanence, and incarnation seem to be the only way in which deity can be conceptualized. As I have already shown, Islam knows God in one of these ways, Judaism knows him in two, and Christianity knows him in all three. This seems to be true of the religions that do not think of God as historically revealed. Insofar as the psychological religions of the East intuit a personal God, it is in the ways we have described.

This is also true of the philosophies that assert the possibility of deity. There are only three systems that men have devised. One is *theism*, which believes in a self-revealing God such as is found in Judaism, Christianity, and Islam. Another is *deism*. The third is *pantheism*.

Deism is an extension-to-impersonality of the transcendence of God. It intuits only the Father. It believes in the possibility of a personal Creator, but it contends that He would have been present only for the creation. He made the universe and ordained laws to keep it in running order; then He went off on a vacation. This is an honest and logical philosophy, but it has no room for grace. It accepts the fact of good and evil, but it makes man wrestle alone with them. Deism's weakness, however, is more than lack of hope; it finally is one of logic. It does not accept the possibility of revelation. It begs the question, "Does God have the *power* to reveal Himself, and to have a hand in the affairs of men?"

Pantheism is an extension-to-formlessness of man's intuition of the Holy Spirit. Its deity is a caricature of the Immanent One in the Godhead. Pantheism thinks of God as being everywhere, and equally available to all. It identifies God so closely with creation that the two become confused: the worshipper tends to become the object of his worship. There is no problem in communication, as there is where man worships an Other. God—or, as is more likely, "the spirit of good"—already fills the worshipper. All the seeker needs to do is to find the key to enlightenment, so that the evil and the unreal may fall away.

Obviously, a pantheistic cult has no need of priesthood or sacraments. These incarnational props are a particularizing of what the pantheist sees as freely available. Nevertheless, a purely immanental religion cannot confer identity, because it rejects the possibility of a real and identifying Other.

Neither deism nor pantheism is helpful in conferring the central traits of personality. Deism denies the possibility of freedom, and sees man as the victim of a predestinating Fate. It cannot hold man accountable for the use of a freedom that he does not have. Pantheism, on the other hand, makes no demands of man, but contends that his every need is met. The grace that the deist does not dream exists becomes, to the pantheist, universally available. Because man is not charged with responsibility, freedom presents no problem. However, when we abandon these philosophies and turn to personal religion, these central traits become a real possibility. They become something that is realized by grace. Man becomes free because God sets him free—on the condition that he be responsible.

Here is the sixth axiom:

Man is personal and triune to the degree that his worship and belief are oriented to the triune personality of God.

If what I have said is true, it is obvious that Christian personality has fallen far short of what it can be. It is also obvious that the worst effect of schism was not what happened to the Church, but what happened to its members. Instead of modeling themselves after God's triunity, they took as their pattern the one Person in the Godhead to whom their churches paid the most attention. The result was not all bad. Many Catholics became saints. Many Protestants became leaders. Pentecostalists became innovators and humanitarians; a few developed genius. However, the bulk of the churches' members became mere caricatures of what they could have been.

Let us stop for a moment to think what this means. A caricature is a quick sketch that shows the subject not as he is, but as the artist chooses to make him appear. The caricature imparts "personality" to the subject by exaggerating a few prominent features. It draws attention to those features at the expense of all the rest. The resulting sketch is not only a *persona;* it is a mask that is put on the subject by someone other than himself. It is not his own *persona* at all. It *imputes*, rather than *reveals*, personal traits.

The splitting of one Church into three churches has led to many caricatures of God. It has led to distortion of each of the Persons, and of their unity as well. More often than not, what men believe about God is only a caricature.

They rarely come face to face with His triune Personality. They mistake the *persona* they have been taught about for that of One who is still largely unrevealed to them. They identify with caricatures, and become caricatures themselves. They are not reshaped by grace into the perfect image of God.

This kind of religion not only frustrates the divine purpose of transforming man's character and personality; it also furthers the schism. Men of opposing faiths, offended by the frauds they see committed, try to set things aright. They endeavor to trace the sketch in its proper proportions, showing God as they think He is. In so doing, they almost inevitably overdo it. They minimize the previously exaggerated features, and concentrate on the ones the previous cartoonist neglected. The result is a new caricature. Action leads to reaction. The conflicting caricatures fall into a pattern of their own—and it is a pattern of threes. It forms a cycle of distortions in the patterns of identity. The cycle that has thus been brought to life distorts not only the triunity of man; it disrupts the divine economy and the vocation of the Church.

The sixth axiom seems to be so self-evident that it hardly needs any proof. Man is in need of the personhood that God projects. Man can have this character if he will identify with the God who *is*—avoiding the temptation to draw and worship a picture. To do this, man must identify with God in all the ways that are given. He must go to God in a *personal* way, using the trinity of forms of worship that Christians have always used. He must identify with God's *will* in the threefold authority-source He has given. If man uses these trinities of worship and belief, he will not want to make caricatures. In faith he will open himself to God, and God will communicate both Himself and His will. Man will not have to draw pictures of God, except for the benefit of those outside the Body. God's self-revelation will be available to the Body and to all its members. This is the process by which man is made triune and by which the Church again becomes one.

The seventh axiom is this one:

God's own triunity suggests that the essential form of social identity is a unity of three—the corporate pattern of the Son, the individual pattern of the Father, and the other-seeking pattern of the Holy Spirit.

Even if we accept the Church's teaching about God's triunity, this axiom is far from self-evident. It takes a little thought to see why a God who is Incarnate must be the basis for corporality, why One who is Transcendent must provide the pattern for individuality, and why an Immanent Other is the prototype for identification with people who are outside the fold.

Let us, therefore, begin with the facts. The churches that have taken their authority and worship from God the Son are the only ones that have provided corporality throughout the Christian centuries. I refer to the catholic churches both of the East and of the West. The same has been true of the Hebrew's priestly religion, whose effects continue still. The identity-symbols, both of Judaism and of Catholic Christianity, have been those of corporate personality. Their community structures have been tribal. In the Christian era it has been only the catholic churches that have maintained their members' corporality when their cultures have ceased to be tribal.

To continue, the churches that have been Father-oriented are the only ones that have developed individuality to a very high degree. (Exception: the Spirit-oriented sects continued it by beginning where an authoritarian individualism left off.) We are limited here, of course, by the fact that modern individualism has been widespread only in the Protestant West. Nevertheless, it can be appreciated that *transcendence is detachment.* Transcendence goes hand in hand with individualism. It puts emphasis upon separation-from-the-group, rather than upon involvement-with-the-Body (which is corporate identity) or with involvement-with-those-outside-the-group (which is the identity-form of the Spirit). A proof of this may be seen in that Father-oriented Islam is also an individualistic religion. Even though Islam is without an adequate theology for freedom and responsibility, and even though its culture has not provided the mechanics for individuation, there is a green light to *personal detachment.* The religions of the East, by contrast, do not encourage this kind of detachment; they provide a *mystical detachment.* Islam stresses the transcendence both of God and man. Like Judaism and Protestant Christianity, Islam fosters individualism by being a religion of a book. Even more than these religions, it is a cult without a priest.

There can hardly be any question that identification-with-others is rooted in the Immanent Person of the Godhead. The Quakers and the Unitarians have shown, more than other Protestants, a concern for those who are outside the area of personal involvement. So have the Jews, who, we must remember, are immanental as well as transcendental. This is also true of the Pentecostal sects, whose tithing and personal commitment have contributed greatly to mission. Over the centuries, however, the greatest missionary body has been the Roman Catholic Church, whose immanentism I have already remarked upon. By contrast, the least successful missionary churches have been the Orthodox. These have emphasized the incarnate and the transcendent in God, but they have been little empowered either by the Spirit-of-change or by the Spirit-of-involvement-with-others.

This sums up the patterns of identity that God has and projects to man. All are meant for man, and all can be had—in varying degree—by identifying with God. Perfection in these, of course, can be seen only in the Person of Christ. He alone, of the men on earth, has shown perfect union of leader, saint, and genius. His character was not limited to the filial traits that we ascribe to His Sonship. He spoke and acted, "not as one of the scribes,"* but with the full authority of the Father. He showed the perfect freedom and other-orientation that we ascribe to the Holy Spirit. This, in fact, is what has led the radical theologians to speak of Jesus as "the man for others."

There is little question that the world itself is in a mood

*Mark 1:22 (AV)

to divinize the spirit-of-change and the spirit-of-concern-for-others. Especially among the young and intellectually ambitious, there is a search for new forms of life in community. Nevertheless, I must insist that Christ is a man for men because of His triunity. If He were not *more* than One who is open to others, He would not be *the* man among men. Jesus can be seen as the Christ because—among other things—he shows forth the perfection of all three forms of social identity. He is triune in Himself, as well as in company with the Father and Holy Spirit. As Paul says, "In him dwelleth all the fulness of the Godhead bodily."*

So long as man has this Pattern to follow, he can appreciate that wholeness in identity is more than a choice of caricatures. It is more than a picking and choosing among trinities, all of which are finally one. The Pattern for men is One who is known as the Son of man and the Son of God. Having this knowledge, each man on earth can find that his own true identity is nothing less than that of a son and likeness of God.

*Col. 2:9 (AV)

Chapter Eight

THE EFFECT OF SYMBOLS
AND SYMBOLIC BEHAVIOR

An age-old complaint about "organized religion" is that its rituals and beliefs are artificial, and thus make hypocrites of those who use them. This is not only nonsense, it shows little understanding either of God or of man, and it is the hoariest of all excuses for avoiding involvement with God.

There is no such thing as a religion without formality. Were there such a thing, it would not be a *personal* religion. All personal religion requires symbolism, both in belief and in expression. Even a Quaker's religion is formal; it merely calls for a different kind of formality than that of the Calvinist or the Catholic. It is a formality that is appropriate to One—but not to the other Two—of the Persons of the Godhead.

Men use symbols and ceremonies because they must. Even when they are engaged in thought, they use symbols that have been stored away in their memories. These symbols may be, and usually are, tokens of experienced reality. They serve in a way that is denied to reality itself. The mind cannot store realities, which are objective and exterior things. But it does hold a vast assortment of percepts and concepts, most of which point to reality. Virtually all these things are stored in symbolic form, which, while it dilutes or re-presents reality, does not necessarily do it an injustice. Rather, it helps men approach reality with greater facility than other creatures, with corresponding benefit to themselves.

The most common symbols are words, which are representatives of the realities they describe. Words are seldom adequate, however, for good communication. This is partly because they have been arbitrarily chosen by the people who use them, rather than allowed to flow from the realities themselves. Because of this, there is an inevitable language barrier between one set of word-symbols and another.

Manners: Signs of Intention

There is another form of symbolism that is more important than words—at least, for personal growth. This is *symbolic behavior*, or *manners*. Manners are "body English." They consist chiefly of physical postures, gestures, and facial expressions. Manners put a higher value upon appearance than upon words. They pay more attention to what the eyes show than to what the lips say. They reveal, better than words are able to do, the secret intentions of the heart.

In an age that tends to neglect behavior, it is significant that social scientists have renewed an interest in manners. They do not refer to them by that term, however, but as *nonverbal communication*. Their interest in manners lies chiefly in what they can teach us about the arts of communication and relationship. Yet the most significant thing about manners is the way they transform people. To use the theological terms of the last chapter, manners give value to personal transcendence. In an immanental age, when familiarity rather than reserve is the keynote, and when equality demands the wiping away of distinctions between people, manners are important, for they alone confirm the integrity of the individual.

Like most other training, the teaching of manners belongs to childhood. Manners need to be taught because, like good intentions, they are not natural to man. Both intention and its symbolic expression become degraded unless they are set straight by training and example.

Functions of Symbols

Let us backtrack for a moment, to get at the meaning of symbols and symbolic behavior. One function of symbols is to describe a reality that is otherwise beyond understanding. A map is purely symbolic, and serves such a purpose. Another purpose of symbols is the mental grasp of abstractions. The multiplication table is such a symbol. It is the kind that, like words, has to be committed to memory in order to have any value.

The highest purpose of symbolism is to convey the life and power of personality itself. This is the point where the symbol ceases to be merely symbolic. It becomes something more; it conveys the thing it signifies. Take, for example, the handshake and the smile. These are symbols in that they betoken friendship, but they are more than that: they are also *acts* of friendship—the very means by which friendship is allowed to grow. We may also say of a kiss that it is a token of love and affection. But it is more: it is the means by which the love is conveyed. In this respect, the kiss transcends symbolism without ceasing to be symbolic.

There is a big difference between those things that are only symbolic and those that are something more. We are seldom bothered about the symbols that deal only with knowledge; on the other hand, we are often concerned about those things that have the power of conveying the thing they symbolize. This is because they deal with intention. We can never be sure that the way people behave toward us is a true sign of the way they feel, yet it has—usually—to be left at that. Only when we accept these symbols at face value can faith have its inning. A handshake does not guarantee friendship. No more does a kiss certify love. They are, however, the proper means by which friendship and love are betokened and communicated. To prove the point, a man can kiss his wife without loving her, but he cannot love his wife without kissing her.

To further prove the necessity of acts that symbolize intention, let me take the simplest kind of communication: that between infants and their mothers. Everyone knows of the tragic things that happen when mothers fail to give outward and visible signs of love to their babies, and when they fail to respond to the babies' own ways of communicating. The baby's cry is a symbolic act. It says, "Do something. Help me." When a baby's mother does not respond to these cries, it gets no sense of success in making its wants known. When its efforts to communicate are regularly ignored, the baby falls into despair and into an autistic withdrawal from reality.

Men's case before God is the same as that of infants before their mothers. They have need for signals from God for the same reason that they have need for signals from one another. That God has given such signals is no indication of any peculiarity on His part. How else than by outward and visible signs of His intention can man be sure of God? Because of man's own psychic need, God has sent forth His symbolic Word. But even this is not enough. Words do not satisfy babies' needs, and they are not a sufficiency for men. For this reason, God has given Himself in Sacrament as well as in Word. In communicating His intention in *behavioral* as well as in *verbal* terms, God has come to man in terms man can understand.

The reason some people question the rites of "organized religion" is that symbolic behavior can be deceitful. It is no matter. This only applies to men's relations with one another. We cannot fool God with our church-manners; He knows the secrets of our hearts. We also can be sure that He has no intention of deceiving us. This is why we can be free from self-consciousness in God's presence, and why we can use joyfully the rites and ceremonies He has given us. Even if we do not understand all that He intends in them, they are bound to be relevant to our needs.

Meaning of God-Given Symbolism

But what about the intention that God may indeed have in these rites and ceremonies? What can they mean? How can they convey, like a kiss, the thing that they signify? Let us consider the possibilities of grace in two rites that Jesus commanded—Baptism and the Eucharist. Let us consider how they may be related to one another, and to the larger purposes of God. Regardless of what men may take them to be, these two rites must have an intrinsic meaning in themselves. They are givens, partly because they are commanded by God and partly because they have a universal meaning.

Since symbols of intention have the power of transcending symbolism, Baptism must be more than a belief-symbol whose only power is what men impute to it. Holy Communion must be more than a mere memorial. All of the God-given rites must transcend symbolism in conveying the life and the love that God intends them to convey. Jesus suggested such a thing when he said to the Samaritan woman at the well,

> Everyone who drinks of this water will thirst again, but whoever drinks of the water that I shall give him will never thirst; the water that I shall give him will become in him a spring of water welling up to eternal life.*

Likewise, Jesus intended for the Eucharistic elements a reality that transcends the significance that we normally give to bread and wine.

> Unless you eat the flesh of the Son of man and drink his blood, you have no life in you; he who eats my flesh and drinks my blood has eternal life, and I will raise him up at the last day. For my flesh is food indeed, and my blood is drink indeed. He who eats my flesh and drinks my blood abides in me, and I in him.†

To discover what Christ meant here, let us think of what bread and wine and water mean in themselves. Then let us see how these meanings have been incorporated into the biblical tradition of the Old Israel and the New. Bread and wine have only one use: they are to be eaten and drunk. They are to be used in meeting man's needs. Perhaps, as with Melchizedek's sacrifice, they may appropriately be offered to God. These elements give nourishment and

*John 4:14 (RSV)
†John 6:53-56 (RSV)

refreshment. They were made "to gladden the heart of man."* They renew life; they give new growth; they supply the energy by which the human organism does its work.

Water, by contrast, has many uses. It refreshes and it cleanses. It gives birth and it can give death. Carried on its surface, man is borne to distant lands. All these meanings are signified in Baptism, and each has an Old Testament figure. One is the ocean of the primal world, out of which came the earliest life.† This is a birth that is repeated in each of us as we leave the watery life of the womb and emerge into the air *(pneuma)* of freedom. Baptism is our cleansing, and it reminds us of Naaman the leper's cleansing in the River Jordan.‡ It refreshes us, as the children of Israel were refreshed by the water that burst from the rock in the wilderness.** It signifies our undoing, as water was the undoing of those who perished in the Deluge. Water is the element that bears up the Ark of our Salvation, as Noah's Ark bore the eight whom he had rescued from the Flood.††

All these are signified in Holy Baptism. It is a rite to which the Old Testament figures point. In baptism we are cleansed from our sins. We die to the old Adam and are reborn to the new man, Christ. Being set free from the past, we are enabled to live vitally in the present. Being incorporated into Christ as a branch is into a tree, we are refreshed by the life that flows from Him to us. We are able to bear His fruit.

Baptism does the same thing for Christians that the Exodus did for the Jews: it brings them into a new life and into a new relationship with God. Paul has suggested the meaning of this relationship in describing the Red Sea as the birth canal of Israel,

> All our fathers were under the cloud, and all passed through the sea; and all were baptized unto Moses in the cloud and in

*Ps. 104:15 (RSV)
†Gen. 1:20
‡2 Kings 5
**Exod. 17:1-7
††Gen. 6-9

> the sea; and all did eat the same spiritual meat; and did all
> drink the same spiritual drink: for they drank of that spiritual
> Rock that followed them: and that Rock was Christ.*

Baptism is an initiation and an engraftment into Christ.
Communion is a feeding upon the life that is in Him. This
is the nourishment that is needed by the man who has
been reborn in the Spirit. To use another figure, Baptism is
the marriage rite in which the Church—the Bride of
Christ—is wedded to her Lord. The Eucharist is the act of
sacred union between the Bridegroom and his Bride.

Symbols? To be sure. But they are more than that; they
are symbolic acts that convey the thing they suggest. They
confer life, power, knowledge of the truth—all the graces
that are needful for the only real life. These graces enable
men and women to grow up into Christ, and so to become
real in themselves.

Transcendent Cultural Symbols

Knowing this, we should give some further thought to
the nature of transcendent symbols. Not all are divine.
Most, in fact, are man-made. Men devise them in the hope
that they will give life to their institutions, and points of
reference upon which members can anchor their own identities. These symbols differ from God's in that they cannot
give the qualities they suggest. They cannot be means of
grace, therefore they become ends in themselves. Such
symbols—whether the logotype, the band uniform, the
salute, the flag, the fasces, the hammer and sickle, or the
clenched fist—tend toward idolatry. None is life-giving.
They demand man's devotion—and sometimes their lives—
without being able to supply more than a framework for
social order.

Function of Symbols in the Divine Economy

Man-made symbols, however, have a value that transcends that of the things they serve. In an institutional

*1 Cor. 10:1-4

setting, they are only idols. In the economy of God, however, they are something more: they are a training device, essential to the development of social character. Men's symbols serve their societies in the same way that a little girl's doll serves its owner. The doll has no material value, yet the little girl imputes the highest kind of value to it. This, if you will, is idolatry. It is something that would grieve us if we should learn that the child were more affected by the loss of the doll than, say, by the death of her mother. Yet, in the divine economy, that doll has a very high value indeed. In playing with it, the little girl trains herself in the motherly concerns that will one day be so important. Her future character is shaped in the make-believe of symbolic behavior and intention.

All people understand that childish play is a preparation for the realities of adulthood. What is not so apparent is that the symbols and institutions of *adult* life are also a form of play. They, too, are a preparation for the future. The connection between men's institutions and the divine plan is shown in Jesus' Parable of the Unjust Steward. In it Jesus was referring to the uses of wealth—what the King James Bible calls "the mammon of unrighteousness." Yet the teaching can be applied to all man's institutions and concepts and symbols. It can be applied to the things men idolize, such as physical perfection, sex, and power.

> My counsel to you is, make use of your base wealth to win yourselves friends, who, when you leave it behind, will welcome you into eternal habitations. He who is trustworthy over a little sum is trustworthy over a greater; he who plays false over a little sum, plays false over a greater; if you, then, could not be trusted to use the base riches you had, who will put the true riches in your keeping? Who will give you property of your own, if you could not be trusted with what was only lent you?*

Jesus looked at all of man's activities as shadows that point to a future reality. He did this because he had a knowledge of personality as extending beyond the grave.

*Luke 16:9-12 (Ronald Knox translation)

He saw man's existence as one of metamorphosis. Man is an acter-with-God in a *here* that ends in the cocoon of death. His continuum then becomes that of a chrysalis in a hidden state of transition. One day his personality will unfold in a resurrection state for which the *here* has been a preparation. In such a frame of reference, man's symbols and institutions play their part. It is true, as we have seen, that they can be a cause of idolatry. But seen from a larger perspective, man's institutions and symbols need no longer be idols. They provide a part of the stage setting within which man's character is tested and transformed.

Dissolution of Transcendent Symbols

All of this has been self-evident to Western man in the past. In the present, however, transcendent symbols—God's as well as man's—seem to be dissolving. Because they are disappearing from sight, many are contending that they always were irrelevant. This is particularly true of the random-directed young. To give an example, the New Left of random-direction is as much set against the communist symbols as it is against those of the free world. This is because random-directed people, being against *all* the symbols that give shape to identity, will not identify with even the revolutionary institutions. Their thought is existential and asymbolic. They seek to recover the innocence and freedom of the undomesticated animal, which has no transcendent symbols to give it shape.

Social science has had a large part in this process. It has fostered random-direction by its assumption that man's transcendent symbols cannot be recovered, and by its decision to create an unstructured identity that has no conscious need for symbols. It has encouraged such a frame of mind by trying out various modes of life-in-the-group. Some of these have already been described—progressive education, sensitivity training, and group therapy. Other modes include the encounter group, the experimental liturgy, and the theatrical technique of audience-involvement. All are intended to set men free from tradi-

tional forms of thought and behavior, and to increase the
individual's adaptability to what is going on around him.
Despite the props, Western man remains confused. He now
has no symbols by which to describe himself. He no longer
uses either God's symbols or his own. What to do? He can
either "accept and adjust," and be swept away in the tide
of random-direction; or he can do what common sense
says he ought to do—use the symbols that are the givens of
his culture, recover his faith in God and in himself, and so
be restored to identity.

It is a curious thing that, even in the ages of faith,
Western man was never more than half aware of his transcendent symbols. That is a part of their value. Unlike
words and concepts, they do not have to be stored in the
conscious mind. They do not, like the flag, have to be paid
attention to in order to be meaningful. The symbols that
are really *given* have a way of rooting themselves in the
subconscious mind, and of staying in the background of
men's thought. This is their proper place. The subconscious is the best place for the things that men feel most
deeply about, and which they are reluctant to discuss.
Words have always seemed too cheap to use in referring to
God, country, family, honor, and truth. The only way men
have ever found to express their feelings about such inti-
mate things has been the way of symbolic behavior. Ceremony does what words cannot do.

It may seem inconsistent to state that men are utterly
dependent upon symbols, and then to point out that the
thought of random-direction is asymbolic. There is no
inconsistency. It is only *transcendent* symbols that are
rejected by random-direction. There are an enormous number of symbols that random-direction accepts without
demurral. They are the ordinary symbols that are used in
everyday communication. These symbols have nothing to
do with social personality. While random-direction denies
the value of symbols that convey identity, it still has to use
the kind that convey meaning. The random-directed man
must use words, and he must engage in abstraction. But he
fights shy of symbols that transcend the here and the now.
This is his way of fighting shy of the institutions that these

symbols point to—whether they be organizations, customs or values.

In order that my remarks about symbolism may seem to make a connection between the identities of God and man, let me distinguish between transcendent symbols and the ordinary symbols that we put to daily use. The first have to do only with social personality; the second have to do with everything else but. To distinguish the one from the other, let us call the ordinary symbols *immanental.* This stretches the meaning of the word, but it will help us see the difference between ordinary symbols and those that refer to the mysteries of personality.

The immanental symbol stands for nothing but what it obviously suggests. There is no *double entendre.* It has no depth of meaning. If it is a word, it is *only* a word; it conveys thought, but is a shallow expression of intention. If it is a form of symbolic behavior, it chiefly relates to feelings. It is the same kind of symbolism the animal uses. It touches the here and the now.

Here are some immanental behavior-symbols: the greeting, "Hi," the slap on the back, the handshake as it is ordinarily used. At best, these types of symbol only verge on the transcendent. They cannot possibly have the meaning that we see in the primitive rite where men become blood brothers by slashing their palms and clasping hands. They do not offer the promise that is given when a man and a woman join hands and exchange the vows of a lifelong Christian marriage.

When random-directed man limits himself in this way, he is protecting himself from the attachments that transcendent symbols can get him into. Immanental symbols do not link people together except in a vague and universal fashion. Transcendent symbols put them in categories; whether for good or ill, they confer a particularity that random-directed people cannot have and do not want. In restricting himself to immanental symbols, the random-directed man permits himself to be "open," "sensitive," and "aware." In this respect he can be more like the animals than can other types of men. He cannot, however, be as open, sensitive, and aware as are the animals themselves.

Most of the power of man's personhood—and much of the pain as well—lies in the fact that man *has* transcendent symbols. The history of the West has been deeply affected by the use to which they have been put. Sometimes they have been rightly used. More often they have not. In the last chapter I showed how the West has been hurt by the inadequacy of its symbolic understanding of God and of its symbolic response to him. Let me finish this chapter by showing how it has been hurt by its symbolic misunderstanding of itself. I shall refer chiefly to the psychological effect of the West's religious art.

Sacred Art in Churches of the East

I have already shown how the incarnationalism of the Catholic and Orthodox churches has given corporate personality to their members. In large part this is because a profusion of incarnational symbols has enriched their corporality. I have also pointed to weaknesses that these churches have possessed in their understanding of personhood. Catholic identity has suffered from a want of transcendence. Orthodox personality has suffered from a want of immanence. The previous chapter's conclusions were based, however, upon a view of identity that was concerned with the effect of freedom, responsibility, and obedience. Here we are concerned only with the effect of symbols and symbolic behavior.

Of all the sacred art forms, that of Eastern Orthodoxy has accomplished the most for man. This is because the East's art alone is genuinely transcendental, and because the Transcendent Father is the Fount both of Godhead and of personality. The lofty mosaics that the Eastern churches have put in their vaults and apses have lent a sense of the numinous. Even more is this true of their icons. The icon glows with transcendence. It is as different from the immanental sculpture of pagan Greece as it is possible for art to be. The icon touches the worshipper just as he is, in all his incarnate earthiness. It opens for him a dimension of mystery and awe. It gives him a glimpse of holy persons and purposes that are undreamt of in ordinary life. It does not leave him at that, however. It stimulates him into making a mystical and personal response. As a result, the icon clothes the worshipper with the transcendence it depicts.

Orthodox art is traditional, stylized, subjective. It is not wrought by individual artists—as in the West—but by guilds of men who treat their work as a divine vocation. The icon is holy. It is always used for a sacred purpose. To quote St. John of Damascus, it is a window that reveals eternity, "an opening towards the imageless transcendent." In Marshall McLuhan's terminology, the icon is "cool," "low definition," "unfinished." It invites the worshipper to complete the picture, to identify with its holy personalities and to participate in its sacred events.

The icon's perspective is the reverse of that of conventional painting. It portrays the divine figures in the background as much larger than the human figures in the foreground. The perspective thus becomes one that looks outward from the eyes of God. The viewer participates in the transcendent by entering a foreground of greatly reduced dimension. There, in a scale that is proper to humility, he gives honor and glory to a God who is clothed in majesty and power.

The architecture and worship of the Eastern churches achieve the same effect. The *iconostasis*, which is the Western rood-screen fashioned into a veil of concealment, protects the sacred mysteries from the unready and profane. The worshipper can hear the Holy Liturgy, but it is ever beyond his vision. So also is the transcendent stressed in the use of music. There is no room here for organ or other instrument. The only sound is that of the worshippers' voices—lifted up to join those of the heavenly choir.

Sacred Art in the West

By comparison with the East, almost everything that has to do with Catholic symbol and ceremony is immanental.

All is specific and "on the surface." It is still concerned with Christ; that is to say, it is incarnational. But its emphasis is upon the *here*, and not upon the *there*. The Mass has a this-worldly goal; *missa* means *a sending*. Because of this emphasis, the Latin *sacramentum* is an indifferent translation of the Greek *mysterion*. *Sacrament* suggests nothing mysterious: it means *a sacred oath or pledge*. In the Latin Church, the Holy Mysteries are interpreted as having more concern with the divine intention than with the communication of the Divine Personality. This does not affect their reality, of course. Yet while the *sacramentum* conveys the thing it suggests, its psychology is as immanental as that of a kiss.

The sacred art of the West is immanental also. The statues and frescoes of the Latin Church fall far short of the Eastern art in expressing the glory of God. Like the sculpture of ancient Greece—from which, in fact, it is borrowed—it is "hot," "high definition," "filled in." Being three-dimensional, it reveals much and conceals little. It fails to stimulate the worshipper's imagination. It says virtually all there is to say.

The same is true of the Latin Church's architecture and worship. Mystery gives place to sentimentality. Transcendence is swallowed up in immanence. There is no *iconostasis* to protect the people from intruding upon the divine holiness. There is no choir between them and the altar—an arrangement that would have the effect of setting them at a distance. The people are all too near the holy mysteries. The rood-screen hides nothing and the choir is at the back of the church. The lay people can see all and hear all; nothing is hid. Even the priest loses his mystery; he is merely an extension of the congregation. If, as is now being done, he goes behind the altar, the altar becomes an extension of the dining room table. If, as is also being done, the priest speaks in a familiar style, even that element of tradition is lost. The Divine Liturgy becomes the Lord's Supper. Theologically it is all quite proper; but psychologically, no. So far as *mystical* involvement is concerned, the effect upon the beholder is nearly neutral. The worshipper has little to do. His imagination is not greatly quickened. He is not asked to project himself towards an ineffable Godhead. He has no transcendent gaps to fill. He is only a passive spectator at the sacred feast.

Of the two churches, the Eastern gave the more secure sense of identity to its members. The Orthodox Church clung to an incarnational view of man, and yet it stressed the transcendent. As a consequence, the East never had a Reformation that matched the one in the West. Nor did its various schisms amount to much; they were concerned with theory, and they hardly touched the people. The transcendental emphasis of Eastern art and liturgy was able to give the Orthodox Christians a good and a fairly constant degree of personal triunity.

The Reformation's Effects on Social Identity

To what degree can our present crisis in identity be attributed to the immanentism of the Western Church? There is a close connection. The final effect of the Reformation was not to restore the transcendence that had been lacking during the Renaissance. It was to make transcendence only a passing phase—and that because of the reformers' rejection of incarnation. The reformers were quite right in using the Bible and the Office to reemphasize the transcendence of the Father. But they made the great mistake of neglecting the symbols and the symbolic behavior that are appropriate to the worship of a Father who dwells in Trinity. As a result, the reformers' children failed to preserve the Reformation.

The tragedy that we are now able to see is that the reformers led their churches into a symbolic wasteland. Partly because the reformers knew very little about the Church in the East, they had to act largely on hunch. As a result they put an end to the incarnational symbolism that would have protected their churches' corporality. Presumably they did this because Latin immanentism had been associated with incarnationalism, so that *both* were regarded as erroneous. The result was a nearly total abandonment of tradition. The reformers threw out the ancient concepts of Church, priesthood, and apostolic order. They dispensed with the sacraments, liturgies, and creeds. As a result, they not only gave an unwitting stimulus to the religious cycle of identity. They set up a vacuum in which the best symbols of the faith must ultimately disappear.

Because of this, the reformers made it impossible for transcendence to take precedence over immanence in the life of man. All symbols and all symbolic behavior were suspected to be idolatrous. The only symbols that were permitted were those of biblical imagery. As a result, many generations of Protestants were reared with few transcendent symbols with which to identify themselves. When the time came that Protestants no longer read the Bible—and no longer were able to think biblically—even *those* symbols disappeared.

As I have pointed out before, all symbolism is ultimately rooted in the natural world. The Creator himself can be understood only in terms of creation. Our difficulty in knowing the Father and the Spirit lies chiefly in that there are so few symbols describing the Two. The only really adequate symbols for the Father are the revealing sunburst and the concealing cloud of glory. The only biblical symbols for the Spirit are the descending dove, the cloven tongues of fire, and the rushing mighty wind. Even the latter are transcendent symbols. An "immanental" symbol cannot truly describe the one Immanent Person of the Godhead because, ultimately, He is as transcendent as the others. It is only His world—and His presence in that world—that can really be thought of as immanent.

Richness in personhood comes with incarnational symbols. These alone are truly descriptive of man. Yet religion itself proceeds from the transcendent. A personally satisfying faith must begin with an appeal to transcendence. It must be fulfilled, however, in producing a devotee in whom transcendence and immanence are incarnated. Let me show how this process has occurred in the past, and then also how it has failed to occur.

Effects of Predestinarian Religion

Most of the great movements in personal religion have been initiated through a leader whose monotheism reacted strongly against the paganism of an immanental world. The first such movement of which we have knowledge was that of Hebrew religion. The transcendence that God revealed to Abraham and Moses* was so power-giving that it enabled a rabble of slaves to win a Promised Land. A second such thrust was that of Muhammad. His reaction was against the paganism of a dying Empire and against the polytheism of his fellow tribesmen then living in Arabia. The third was that of John Calvin. A fourth was that of Karl Marx. Each of these movements was predestinarian. Each gave its adherents the conviction of being saved. Along with that conviction there came an enormous release of personal power—of selfless immersion in a cause. In each of these cases it was a power that swept all before it until some of the movements' internal weaknesses had come to light, and until their initial enthusiasm had dissipated.

Even though the last of these faiths is atheistic, all are genuine religions. (Communism, like the others, is rooted in a single principle of law and order.) Each created its own forms of identity with a set of transcendent symbols. Each protected itself by proscribing the use of conflicting symbols. Each found the puritan ethic vital to its cause.

There is an important way in which the puritanism of a predestinarian religion touches upon the identity crisis of our time, namely, in its effect upon symbolic art. Like predestination itself, it finds its inception in the religion of the Hebrews. Specifically, it begins with the commandment against the worship of idols.† Both Abraham and Moses had seen the abominations that people commit when they do not have a Transcendent Other as the governor of their lives. Yet despite the power of the Hebrews' puritanism, their incarnationalism was never

---

*Earlier, we saw how Yahweh showed forth the divine immanence. So far as the Hebrews were concerned, however, that quality touched only themselves. They thought of Yahweh's will for other peoples as one of predestined failure. When the Jews called themselves a *chosen* people, it was in the same sense as the Calvinist *saved.*

†Exod. 20:4,5

quenched. They never lost their delight in nature. They never lost their ability to bend nature itself to the worship of their God. As a result, they did not interpret the Second Commandment as forbidding the *making* of graven images. They simply could not *worship* those images. The Ark itself was shielded with the graven wings of cherubim. The Temple was decorated with figures of men and angels, and of plants and animals.

The Muslims were far more austere both in their puritanism and in their predestinarianism. They interpreted the Second Commandment as forbidding any likeness. They limited their art therefore to geometric designs. This is one reason why the Arabs became individualists, and why they were able to pass some of their culture to the Renaissance West. Being abstracted from nature, they developed an interest in mathematics and philosophy. Having this—as well as having their own form of the Bible and Office— they developed a form of identity that was relatively detached.

In its distaste for symbolism and for showy forms of worship, the puritanism of the Reformation went beyond that of Islam. The Muslims, in their art and architecture, had made up in design and color what they lacked in symbolic form. Moreover, they had an incarnational concept of life. They showed a high degree of naturalness in their ethics. Self-denial was not an important feature of their religion. By comparison, the Christian puritan was inhibited both in his thinking and in the way he spoke and behaved. His art tended to be colorless and unimaginative. The worst feature of puritan life, however, was the character of his worship. The church manners of Calvinism were more appropriate to the worship of an indwelling Spirit than to that of a far-away Father. The puritan seemed to sit in contemplation of a God Within, rather than of an External Other. In his symbolic behavior, at least, the Muslim was on safer ground. While he did not have as great an opportunity as the Calvinist for personal fulfilment, he at least was able to prostrate himself to the ground in his worship of Allah. Whatever psychic benefit he could obtain from such worship, he obtained it to the full.

In his way, the communist is also puritan. Like the Hebrew, the Muslim, and the Calvinist, he is subordinated to the grand design of an overpowering autonomy. He differs from the earlier puritans largely in that he is wholly this-worldly. He is entirely immanental in his field of interest and concern. The only transcendent element in his faith is its overriding purpose, which transcends—or is supposed to transcend—the total life of man. Like the other predestinating faiths, it has had to put away all lesser loyalties, and to drive out all transcendent symbols that are not its own. But the symbols it has substituted have no real value at all. As a result, the men that communism creates are not truly men.

It is unfortunate that the reformers, in seeking to renew transcendence, chose the right forms of worship and authority to achieve their end, but neglected to use the appropriate forms of symbolism and art. This has happened before, however, and it can happen again. Whenever transcendence is emphasized as a reaction against polytheism, there is a reduction of symbols. Abraham reacted against temple prostitution. Muhammad reacted against fellow Arabs who worshipped the sun and the moon and the stars. Calvin reacted against the seeming polytheism of Renaissance Rome. Marx reacted against the seeming polytheism of nineteenth-century capitalism. In all these cases their crusades were met with outward signs of success, yet all were conducted at the expense of the transcending symbols of life.

A few churches in the West have kept a measure of transcendence, and have passed it along to their members. These churches, as it happens, did not originate with Latin Christianity, but had their earliest roots in the East. Among them are the Anglican and Irish Catholic churches, and also the Lutheran churches of northern Europe and the Catholic churches of northern France and the Low Countries. All can be called Gallican, rather than Roman, in their earliest geneology. All find their origins in the missionary work of Jewish Christians who went from Palestine to France and Britain in the first century. Their earliest roots of custom and tradition lie with the Johannine Church of the East rather than the Petrine Church of the West.

Immanental Mood of Western Churches

Even in these churches, however, transcendence is fading away. This is largely because of the West's preoccupation with this-worldly concerns. Both scientism and welfarism are immanental. The science of psychology, especially, has reduced transcendence to a lost dimension. Nothing is any longer "sacred." That is to say, there is nothing that others cannot pry into. Nothing is allowed to be kept hidden and undisclosed.

The tragedy of the Western churches—and this includes Catholics as well as Protestants—is that they they have acquiesced to the immanental demands and mood of the world. I am not referring to the immanentalism that is shown in their social concern. Here, at least, they are respecting the ethical demands of Old Testament justice. Rather, the churches are showing their lack of transcendence by grasping for the same things that the world is seeking. Many are experimenting with group dynamics. Many are venturing much in the liturgies they try. Many are seeking as avidly as pagans for unstructured forms of identity. They are groping as blindly for new and "meaningful" forms of morality.

This kind of foolishness is very evident to those who remain outside the Church, and who nevertheless know what identity is. The Church is the guardian not only of a revelation that has shown the structures and values of human life, but also of the symbols and symbolic expressions that are essential to that life. Not all the churches, fortunately, are trying to find identity by breaking loose from their moorings, but only the collectivist churches—those that have forsaken Scripture and Tradition in favor of "holy" reason. It is a tribute to the common sense of Judaism that none of the synagogues in America has experimented with group behavior. Where Jews have engaged in "encounter," it has been entirely apart from the cultic life.

There is a good deal of evidence, however, to show that men are trying individually to find the very dimension that institutionally they are rejecting. The mystical flight to the East is one such bit of evidence. Another is the current experimentation with sex and drugs. A third is the return, after several centuries, of the age-old mystery religions—the occult arts and witchcraft. It does not really matter that all these things are immanental, for they show that modern man is unfulfilled by the forms of immanentism he has and is trying to burst the bounds—to find something he does not understand and can never know. In a world that is saturated with itself, he is searching for another.

What does matter is that man can never find transcendence except in finding the Transcendent. He cannot even search except by using the means that are given. Man's only lasting shape is the triune shape of God. Man needs individuality as well as corporality. He needs detachment as well as involvement. He needs responsibility and obedience as well as freedom. He needs the symbolic forms of behavior that can help develop these things.

All these qualities are developed in a relationship with a God whose first dimension is transcendence. They are found in an *involvement* that requires *detachment* from the world. Man's knowledge both of God and of himself begins with his use of the symbols that God has given. The quality of his response to that gift—that is to say, the quality of his symbolic behavior—will demonstrate, as nothing else can, the grace that has flowered within.

Chapter Nine

THE ECONOMICS OF SOCIAL PERSONALITY

We begin now to draw together some of the themes that have been developed in the course of these chapters. While the last three have been devoted to religion, we must not forget that our primary concern is social personality. We are dealing chiefly with the great elements of freedom and responsibility, as they touch man's concept of self and society. We are also concerned with the realities of life and power, both in the individual and in the group.

I have traced the evolution of four concepts of identity. In so doing, however, I have pointed out that they are not actually four, but three. These are the corporate, individual, and collective (or universalist) views of man. I have also suggested how these three are derived from the identity of a triune God, who has given man the forms of identity that exist within Himself.

It seems obvious that the last of these three forms—the universal—is based upon a false intuition of God the Holy Spirit. Even though it apprehends the qualities that the Spirit supplies, it is a caricature of the real. It visualizes a *Persona* instead of a Person. It will be the purpose of this chapter to find a truer doctrine of the Spirit, and to describe the identity it suggests for man.

The secular cycle of identity is an inevitable accompaniment to the rise and fall of a culture, and in fact *is* the rise and fall. The vitality that men acquire when they become individual persons is what gives power to an emerging society. The reduction of power that marks a return to the group *is* the culture's decline. At every point in a people's evolution, religion can protect them against loss of identity and decline in power. At least, this is so where there is *personal* religion. Where religion itself is impersonal, very little help is given. The culture may indeed experience a rise and a fall, but there will have been very little emergence. Personhood will not really have flowered at all.

This means that we are dealing chiefly with the cyclical changes that have been going on in the Judeo-Christian world. Apart from the faiths that grew out of Abraham's, there has been no personal religion; and even they have been unable to save the West. When Christendom was divided by schism, a cycle of identity was set up that had not existed before. As it has turned out, this religious cycle has left Christians nearly as vulnerable to the secular cycle as are those who have no religion. This was not so self-evident when the religious cycle was accenting the personhood of the Father and the Son. However, now that the secular and the religious cycles are phased in on the properties of the Spirit, the weakness is painfully obvious.

In speaking as I have of the Spirit and His properties, I do not mean to be irreverent. Collective personality may indeed show an intuition of the Spirit's intent to universalize the identity of man, but it misreads the form and the functions of the personhood He projects. Collectivism is an identity-form that pays attention to the Spirit without letting itself be shaped and enlivened by the Spirit. It is only a caricature of the divine—the most shapeless of all forms of identity.

Here is the danger in our culture's stress upon the immanent and upon the other attributes that we ascribe to the Spirit: emphasis upon these qualities *detracts* from corporate and individual personality. It does not create a real other-orientation, but merely fosters other-direction. It forms a diffuse and unlocalized sense of identity. As such, it has nothing to do with the *Person* of the Holy Spirit. It stresses His attributes, but it loses sight of *Him*. It entirely overlooks His functions.

The primary function of the Spirit is to draw men to the Father and the Son. Psychologically, this implies that freedom exists in order that men may grow in responsibility and in voluntary obedience. However, when people covet the Spirit's attributes without accepting His functions, they are impeding their own personal growth. In seeking the universal rather than the particular, they are concerning themselves only with the Spirit's secondary function. That function is to identify Christians so greatly with the *other* that the Church may become the instrument for bringing all mankind into the family of God. The collectivist's failure is this: in not allowing the Spirit to exercise His primary function of giving corporality and individuality, sympathy becomes empathy, the self is blended with the other, personhood is lost, and the divine economy is unfulfilled.

In a Body that is fully the Church there is no reason why, at any stage of the secular cycle, members should not have personal triunity. They have a sufficient knowledge of the form of God's identity. They have the three sufficient sources of divine authority. They have the worshipping response-in-trinity that the human psyche requires. Acting on this understanding, the churches of the West can be the means of remolding their members' identities into the triune image of God. They can also be the means of resurrecting the identity of an otherwise shapeless world.

Unfortunately, it does not seem to be working out that way. The churches are still three—not one. In their efforts to achieve unity they still visualize man as trinity-without-unity. Furthermore, their actions are those of men who act in their own wisdom and strength, rather than in the grace and power of God.

Myths of Collective Identity

By this time, the concepts of collectivism have saturated the Western mind, both inside and outside the Church. So have collectivism's myths, which are increasingly accepted as true. As I have shown, these myths are not truly descriptive of man; therefore they need to be exposed and destroyed.

One such myth is *the involved man.* This is unreal because it denies the dimension that comes from a detached and transcendent Father. It overlooks the need for a dynamic of detachment *and* involvement, which alone permits a man to have both corporality and individuality. It points to the ultimate myth of *total involvement,* which justifies every encroachment into private life including brainwashing.

Another such myth is *the homogenized man.* This is a variant of the ancient *scandal at particularity,* which contends that differences are not important. It denies the sacramental principle that God acts in particulars, and that some things can be made holy for the sake of others. Ultimately, it denies that God and man are *trinity.* It demands uniformity as the price of unity.

An illustration of this myth is the evolution of the word *racism.* This word has only recently evolved from an older word, *racialism.* It did not become a dictionary term until the middle 1950s. As *racialism,* it used to signify the kind of prejudice or discrimination that is a mark of racial hostility or a belief in racial superiority. As *racism,* it now contains overtones of *awareness of differences.* Insofar as this is so, *racism* is a meaningless word to all but collectivists. Everyone who shares in corporality has got, by definition, to be a racist. So does every individualist. Each is geared to the idea that differences help to give identity. Whether these people are *racialists,* however, depends upon their training in intention.

Dilemmas of Social Identity

It would seem that man's identity can be completed only by acknowledging the pattern of God's triunity, and by doing so in His power. To allow this is to overcome three dilemmas of identity that, in the past, have rarely been resolved. The first is the dilemma of the secular cycle. Secular man has moved from tribalism to individualism in a pattern of emergence—only to have his selfhood disappear in a collectivist loss of identity. The second is that of Judaism. The Jews have succeeded in achieving a paradoxical identity in which corporality and individuality are combined, but they never shared this identity with the world. Judaism has failed in its vocation to bring the nations into companionship with God.

The third dilemma is that of the Christian Church. It has had the same vocation as the Jews, but has not fulfilled that vocation. Its success in identifying with the "other" has been accomplished at cost to its own identity.

To sum up, the Jews have not wanted to universalize their identity, and the Christians have been unable to. The New Israel, being separated from the Old and being divided within itself, has seldom been able to achieve a personal balance in which corporality and individuality were combined. Even though it was oriented toward an "other," it was relatively impotent. It could not share what it did not have.

Possibilities for Triunity

Here we come face to face with the ultimate riddle of history. How is mankind to acquire a universal identity that is rooted in God's identity, and that will include both a corporate and an individual sense of personhood? There is a twofold answer—one that is rooted in the oldest doctrines of Israel.

The first part of the answer lies in the biblical doctrine of the *remnant*. This idea goes back as far as Noah. It is as essential to the New Testament as to the Old. The remnant is an inner core of faithful people who are used by God to sanctify an otherwise unbelieving world. They are a personal example of the sacramental principle that God works in particulars to achieve a universal result. What the remnant *is* is a self-sacrificing entity. It is one that puts God first, and is wholly devoted to His will. What the remnant *does* will depend upon the nature of the times. In times of spiritual advancement, the remnant is a channel by which the grace of God may be mediated to others. In times of adversity it is an entity whose sole accomplishment is to

196 of 224 The Restless Heart

keep alive the witness of God. At one time it may be the *faithful, righteous, saving remnant.* At another time it will be merely the *preserved.*

Whether in ebb tide or flood, the remnant's task is the same. It is to keep alive the knowledge of God, so that there will never be a time when He is without witnesses on earth. Its function of channeling grace is one that Jesus has described in His teachings. The remnant is the leaven that gives *pneuma* to the loaf. It is the salt that seasons the people's fare.

We can see the remnant everywhere in the life of the Church. Within the Body it is the tiny band of lay people who join the clergy in their daily liturgies and prayers. Out in the world it is the "two or three gathered together" who bring holiness to the life of secular institutions.

In its divinely ordained sense, the remnant is a series of concentric circles. The outer may be virtually congruent with the whole—as the yeast is with the dough. The inner is no more than an entity of one. The Church, for example, is a holy remnant in an otherwise disordered world. This is so in spite of the fact that most of its members are far from holy. Again, in every congregation there is a remnant, which is the salt that seasons its life. Yet most of this remnant's members are far from holy. As it turns out, there are remnants within remnants. Even when the inner remnants are seemingly negligible—as in the time of Moses, Jeremiah, Athanasius, Luther—there is always a smaller core. The remnant has got finally to be centered in Jesus Christ. He is the remnant in its ultimate sense.

Myth of the Liberal Image

At this point we may debunk a third myth—that of *the liberal as the man in the middle.* For decades the liberal's self-image has been that of a mediator between a reactionary right and a revolutionary left. In terms of political reality, this image has often been appropriate. However, if instead of left and right we use the form of trinity, the myth is shown up as nothing but a myth. The liberal is seen to be the only real revolutionary. He will not accept the force of tradition or custom. He will not be an individualist. He cannot be a tribalist.

Part of the liberal's difficulty comes from his own feelings about identity. He underidentifies with his own, and he overidentifies with those who are not his own. The liberal has few defining traits because he is unwilling to adopt what might be regarded as bias. In identifying with others, he moves from sympathy to empathy and beyond. He is marked by what Paul called *pathos*, which in the King James Bible is translated *inordinate affection.* *

It is because of this unwillingness to commit himself to anything that might be called corporate that, when the chips are down, the liberal exposes a want of corporate virtue. When diplomacy has failed, and when those who are his own are suffering from the onslaughts of naked power, the liberal is found lacking in the qualities that then are needed—loyalty, solidarity, and subordination. Having been unwilling to be a part of a tribal group, he is unable to produce its traits when finally put to the test.

In the time of John Stuart Mill the liberal (whom we now call the classic liberal) was a secure and convinced individual who could identify with an "other." He deliberately stood outside all institutions, having the belief that man is basically good and that institutions can only harm him. The modern liberal, by contrast, stands within institutions, and by sheer weight of numbers has come to control them. Still believing that man is basically good, he has converted his institutions to serve something besides the sanctification of man. This is nowhere more apparent than in the collectivist churches. The bodies that used to exist for the transformation of individuals are now dedicated to the reform of society.

The Importance of Observance

The second part of the answer to the riddle of universal identity is something that has always been known to the Jews, but has largely been hid from the gentiles—especially

*Col. 3:5

in the West. This is the understanding that religion is not so much a matter of *belief* as it is of *observance*. George Foote Moore has remarked on this in his classic work on Judaism.[1] Erich Fromm has also spoken of it in *The Art of Loving*, although he phrases it somewhat differently, "The ultimate aim of religion is not the right belief, but the right action."[2]

This is a notion that seems, at first, to be contrary to the Protestant doctrine of justification by faith. Especially is this so when *observance* is interpreted—as I would make it—as *man's worshipping response to the personal outreach of God*. The gentiles' tendency to separate belief from observance is shown in the casual theology of the man in the street. He rationalizes his scorn for symbolic behavior by saying, "It doesn't matter how you worship. The important thing is what you believe." Or, in a variant, "It's not what you believe that matters most with God. It's how you put your belief into practice." The second, of course, is pure nonsense. The Nazis were putting their beliefs into practice very successfully when they herded Jews and gypsies into the gas ovens. Each of these theologies is as cheap as the other. Both try to do what cannot be done— separate creed, cult, and conduct from one another. The first, at least, is "religious"; but it suggests that man's relationship with God is a matter of talking propositionally rather than of acting relationally.

The matter comes into focus when we realize that Luther was not thinking of belief when he spoke of justification by grace through faith. It is true that *pistis (faith)* can mean *belief in a set of religious propositions*. But more importantly it means *trust*. It is not a trust that is faith in faith, but a *personal trust in God*. This kind of faith is a work only when it is the personal work of God.

This means that liturgical observance does not have to be regarded as a work. Much less is it a dead work. It is an outward response of the sort that is necessary to relationship. Moreover, it has a form that is a given. In an earlier chapter I have demonstrated the power of liturgical observance to transform the character of men. This is more than an accident. Liturgy, like faith, is a means of grace. In a psychological sense, it is no more than the appropriate response that man needs to make to God. Theologically, it is one of the profoundest means by which man is shaped in His image.

Fallacies Regarding the Spirit's Work

There are three erroneous ideas of the Spirit's work that may be found in a church that is not acting in His power. They all impede the life of grace that is needed for the Church to fulfil its mission. One is the *exclusive fallacy* that God's intention is limited to an elite who are to be saved. This makes the remnant an end rather than a means. It is a notion that cannot be justified by Scripture; the First Epistle to Timothy tells us that God "desires all men to be saved and to come to the knowledge of the truth."*

A second mistake is the *inclusive fallacy.* This is the belief that men are to be gathered into the fold by every means conceivable, with every possible shortcut. It overlooks that the primary purpose of the Church is to transform human character—a goal for which there can be no shortcuts.

The third is the *fallacy of a single means.* Churches that accept this idea overlook the breadth of the divine economy and the depth of the divine personality. They also assume that the divine-human relationship can be entered into only by those who are still in this life. They ignore the function of a Church in Paradise, which is given the custody of those who have departed this life. This branch of the Church would seem to have the duty to "gather up all the fragments that remain, that nothing be lost."

I believe that a church that overlooks such a possibility is making a serious mistake. It is forced to use the "hard sell" that rams the God-man relationship down men's throats. Much of the Father-hostility that psychiatrists have noted in both Protestants and Catholics has come as a result of "hard sell." The Protestants have not been taught about Paradise. They have been taught a particular judg-

*1 Tim. 2:4 (RSV)

ment that sends men, at their death, either to heaven or hell. Catholics are taught about Paradise, but they learn to call it Purgatory. They believe that no free will exists there, that it is not a place of probation, and that once one is there, it is too late to change one's mind.

The biblical evidence, however, is that there *is* a Paradise, and that in it probation is a possibility, since Jesus won converts there in the two days between his death and his Resurrection.* This has a hopeful meaning for Christians who are charged with spreading the gospel. If they can be assured that God has other means than themselves, and other times than the present, a hopeful note may be added. Their evangel need never sound grim. In giving the "other" more than a semblance of freedom, Christians can add to their other virtues the qualities of lightheartedness and humility. Such traits will surely make them more attractive to those to whom they are sent.

Want of a Theology of the Spirit

All through the Church's history there has been one difficulty: the Church has never acquired an adequate doctrine of the Holy Spirit. In part this is because during the centuries of its unity the Church was occupied in working out its doctrines of Christ and of the Trinity. It never quite got around to the Person and work of the Spirit. Yet the wholeness of man lies as much in his doctrine of the Spirit as in his doctrine of the Church. The Spirit lives and moves in the Church—but not altogether. He gives grace through the Church and its sacraments—but not exclusively. The Church does not *own* the Spirit. She can call Christ her own, for she is His Bride and He her Bridegroom. But she cannot so possess the Father or the Spirit. It is in this sexual symbolism that we can find an answer to this dilemma. When the Church is most truly the Bride of Christ, her gender is feminine—not neuter. The *organic* Body is a She—not an institutional It.

This has something to say about the Church today. A

*Luke 23:43; 1 Pet. 3:18,19; Eph. 4:8-10

body that is highly organized and carefully administered is not the Bride of Christ. It is not even a Body in any viable sense. It is an institutional It that will not allow the She within to emerge. It is an organization that is likely often to be anxious about itself. It is bound to give respect to status, and to deny its lay people their freedom. It is likely to discourage rather than allow polarization. For reasons of face it cannot permit its members, in their disagreements, to be disagreeable. That is to say, they cannot even be themselves. Such a Church cannot permit what is normal in every family—the conflicts that are usually resolved by suffering and forgiveness. It disallows the griping that a good commander encourages in his men.

The myth for the collectivist church is the biblical story of Babel. Men aspired there to power and fame, but instead of gaining it, they were scattered and humiliated. Their speech was confounded, so that—unlike other creatures—they were unable to communicate with their own kind. Here is the myth, not only for the collectivist church, but for every purely human activity.

Possibilities for the Church

By contrast, the possibilities for a *corporate* Church are suggested in the miracle of Pentecost. That happened when the Holy Spirit descended upon Jesus' disciples and gave them the gift of tongues. In the power of the Spirit they poured into Jerusalem's streets, offering glory and praise to God in languages they did not even know. This is an event that betokens the simple and open personhood that existed before Babel, when "the whole earth was of one language, and of one speech."*

Our present reality is very little different from that which existed on the day of Pentecost. The earth is *not* of one language. No earthly power can give it corporality. Yet the greater reality is that these things *may be*, and that they *are already*—in the mind of God. The Pentecost-event is a signpost that points into the future, declaring the

*Gen. 11:1 (AV)

purposes of God. It says that corporality can be extended to all mankind. This corporality, however, is the work not primarily of God the Son, with whom we associate corporality, but of God the Holy Spirit, who brings men of good will to God in the power of their own freedom, moving the Church lovingly and responsibly out to meet them.

Since the work of the Spirit is to bring all men into the fold of Christ, we cannot allow ourselves to forget that the Church is the holiest of the mysteries of man. It is all the more holy because it is destined, some day, to be the home both of the Old Israel and the New. In accepting the Church as an extension of God in history, Christians must give place to the Spirit in order that He may act. The activism must be His—not the Church's.

Dynamics of Family and Home

Let us now turn briefly to the family and the home. Here we must appreciate one thing: even though the family is a divine institution, it does not exist for the same reason as the Church. It has no part in giving a universal identity, but exists rather to give a *particular* identity. It bestows corporality, and it lays the groundwork for individuality. This means that, for a house to be a home, the parents have got to leave their collectivism outside the door. A child is not helped by having parents who believe differences do not matter.

A parent's most important gifts to a child are discipline and love. Even these can be sentimentalized, however. The love that a parent gives a child must gradually become less sheltering. Discipline, too, must change. It must gradually be converted from an exterior force to one that the child imposes upon himself. Together, discipline and love make it possible for the child to acquire by himself what he most needs in order to become an individual: a healthy respect for himself. Self-respect cannot be given, as love and discipline are, but must be earned by the child. This requires the parents' conditional gift of freedom—freedom to *achieve.* A child acquires respect for himself when he has done something that has earned the respect of others. Those others should be his elders and superiors, whose opinions he values and whose examples he tries to follow.

Conscience Formation

Even at an early age, children need to judge themselves. From the time they begin to go to school, they are away from their parents much of the time. Already they are beginning to have multiple associations. This means that their actions need to come under the survey of their own consciences. Since conscience is not an innate gift, but something that is imparted by discipline, its formation is the most central concern of parents. Conscience is formed in the child by teaching and example. It is fixed by careful supervision, with appropriate punishment and rewards.

I have already pointed out that conscience is more important to the released individual than it is to the tribalist. This is a practical matter. The only way an individualist can continue to have a sense of corporality is to carry his community with him in the form of a conscience. Both psychically and ethically, his conscience *is* the group. When the released individual consults his conscience, his basic community is there.

Such a meaning is borne out by the New Testament *syneidēsis*. This is a word all the English translations render as *conscience*. *Syneidēsis* is *a seeing together, a joining together in one view*. When a child has learned to consult his conscience he is sitting in council with all who have ever taught, disciplined, or judged him. He is at one with all who have given him his values and identity.

This means that, for conscience-formation, parental community is a must. So also is the need for consensus. I am speaking not only of couples, but also of whole communities. When two children find that their consciences do not agree, the identity of each is weakened. Especially is this so if both have good intentions. It is because of conflicts in values among parents that conscience has begun to disappear. It is because of permissiveness in homes and schools that children make up values of questionable worth, for which they themselves are the authority.

It is obvious that the only kind of community that can arrive at the values that are needed by conscience is a religious one. Only a church or synagogue can transmit values that are both intrinsic and universal. Yet the transferring of these things to conscience is something that can be done only in the home. If a child does not already have a conscience by the time he arrives in the schools, it is already too late.

Another thing that is essential to the home is the practice of religion. Only in the home can children really find their life-relationship with God. This brings us to the last of Judaism's great secrets—the religious character of the family. The family has always been the heart of Judaism. The vitality of the family has been maintained by appropriate *observance*. This is something that the Christian West once knew, but has recently forgotten.

Use of the Puritan Ethic

All through these pages I have borne down heavily upon the need to perceive intrinsic values, and to relate them to an Other. I do not, however, discount the worth of situational values, or of the way they are arrived at. In fact, I shall suggest a few such values and goals at which the West might profitably arrive.

The only way to make an overpopulated world livable is for the *have* nations to export the puritan ethic to the *have-not* nations. People who have an insufficiency of material things need to acquire a love of work as an end in itself. This cannot be accomplished by give-away programs. It can only be accomplished by the kind of secular mission that sends puritans to the poor. The West can send as missionaries those who can show forth their own love of work, and who can teach their skills to all who will learn. This is the kind of beneficence that has always been seen in Judaism, where the highest kind of charity is regarded as setting another man up in business. Such a deed is good because it helps another to help himself. It gives him pride in achievement, and sets him free from dependence upon another.

Such a program of mission lays upon the West a burden for itself. If the West is going to export puritanism, it has to remain puritan in itself. Yet it must have a *religious*, rather than a *social*, form of puritanism. Unless our puritanism can be transformed into motivations of laboring-with-God-for-the-sake-of-others, it can only continue the form of imperialism that was seen in ancient Rome, and that is so widely seen today.

A religious puritanism will require self-denial in consumption as well as in production. We must end the wasteful use of things that is the only present excuse for extravagance in production. This is a necessity for more than psychological reasons: it is coupled with our need to preserve the environment in which we live.

The psychological necessity of puritanism is important, however. The West needs to give up its household-centered accent on personal comfort. In a society that is choked with the cares and riches and pleasures of this life, there is a vocation for Christians to live a life of holy poverty. Churchmen who are securely God's can begin to reduce their accent on the family symbol. They can begin to think of themselves as a remnant sent to bring life and health to an impoverished world. These people must enlarge their accent on the soldier-symbol. They must learn to live creatively on the edge of poverty. Like soldiers, they must learn to travel light, without encumbering possessions.

The Heritage of Western Identity

The greatest gift the West can make to the rest of the world is the gift of Judeo-Christian identity. It will seem to many to be patronizing to speak of those people as heathen who have never known God through Moses or Christ. Yet there is no question that their social identity has been stunted through their lack of personal religion, as has also their ability to become individuals by responsible use of freedom, and by living in a one-to-One relationship with a grace-giving God.

Our sociologists have made several false assumptions about non-Western identity. One is that the difficulty non-Westerners have in industrializing their economies is due to a social identity that limits their freedom and responsibility. This is true so far as it goes, but it does not go far enough. It makes the effect become the cause. The cause of non-Westerners' difficulty is their want of personal religion. Apart from what they have picked up from Christian missionaries, they have never had the revelation of a personalizing God. They have never quite known what it means to be a free and responsible self.

Klaus Mehnert expresses the sociologists' viewpoint when he comments upon a passage of Ruth Benedict's in her book, *The Chrysanthemum and the Sword*,

> "Where shame is the major sanction, a man does not experience relief when he makes his fault public even to a confessor. So long as his bad behavior does not 'get out into the world' he need not be troubled and confession appears to him merely a way of courting trouble. Shame cultures therefore do not provide for confession, even to the Gods."[3]

> China . . . represents a 'shame culture' as distinct from the 'guilt culture' which is a product of Christianity. One Chinese has in fact explained the relatively small success of Christian missions in China by the fact that missionaries, especially in their Protestant variations, relate everything to personal conscience, and in China, where more importance is attached to shame than guilt, conscience is not greatly developed. In the same way, many sociologists believe the formation of a guilt culture through Christianity to be one of the reasons behind the spiritual and hence the civilizing dynamism of the Occident, whereas in China (and in Asia generally) they see in the priority of shame over guilt a definite factor contributing to the desire for conformity, to be inconspicuous, and inhibiting any wish to stand out as a reformer, let alone a revolutionary.[4]

I have cited this passage for two reasons. One is the extraordinary similarity it suggests between the shame cultures of the East and the anxiety culture of the contemporary West—namely, an unwillingness to confess what is seemingly hidden from sight, a desire to conform to the group and thus to be inconspicuous, and an intense pre-occupation with face.

The other reason is this: it is not true that members of shame cultures are incapable of confession; this is true only where those cultures have no knowledge of a personal God. It is also untrue that guilt culture began with Christianity. The original guilt culture was the Hebrews'—dating back six hundred years before Christ. Yet even they were a shame culture for more than a thousand years after the time of Abraham. During those centuries—and especially after the time of Moses—confession was the very heart of their relationship with God.

What I have said about the gift to the rest of the world of Judeo-Christian identity-concepts disregards two things. First, the West has already been doing this for centuries. Secondly, those concepts are now being lost to the West itself. James Joyce has drawn attention to this in a strange bit of prophecy,

> The silent cock shall crow at last. The west shall shake the east awake . . . while ye have the night for morn.[5]

Despite his prescience, however, Joyce made the same error as the sociologists. He ignored that without the cause—which is personal religion—the effect—which is personal identity—is not exportable. David Riesman made the same mistaken assumption about cause and effect:

> Americans do not realize that all the world is now in on what were once the white man's secret weapons: his character, his values and his organization.[6]

None of these people has stopped to realize that the West's secret weapon has been a personal relationship with God. Without that relationship there could hardly have been the dynamic that gave character and values. Without the character and values there could hardly have been the organization. It takes a genuine religion to give the kinds of tradition that created a stable inner-direction. And it took inner-direction to give the detachment that enabled Western man to dominate his world. It is true that the West has begun to "shake the East awake." That is to say, it has succeeded in getting the East to copy its life-style. But the result is not a real awakening, for it does not involve a transfer of identity. The East will only get another dose of the random-direction into which it has wandered, from time to time, throughout its history.

It appears that the real challenge for the future will be one not so much of the West's exporting its identity as of protecting it. In a world that is seemingly in dissolution, our vocation may not be one of being a saving remnant. It may be that of being the *preserved*. This does not mean that the West has to give up its historic role of world leadership. It means that a West that is in psychological retreat ought to take the time to make a spiritual retreat. The West can hardly give away to others an identity that it no longer has for itself.

Whether we look upon ourselves as a saving remnant or as a *preserved*, Western man has to be true to himself. And by this I do not mean a random-directed, twentieth-century style. We have to be true to the generations of the past as well as to those of the future. Only in this way can we be true to God and ourselves.

Sin and Suffering: a Personalizing View

In back of the confusion on the current scene lie two unwarranted assumptions about man. One is that the individual is not really free, and that he cannot therefore be held accountable. The other is that suffering—not sin—is the paramount evil in life. Both of these notions are in conflict with the Judeo-Christian belief. That is the knowledge that man is free and that sin is not only the root evil, but the cause of most of man's suffering.

It is a remarkable fact that only under the auspices of Judaism and Christianity has human suffering been successfully dealt with. Eastern religions, by contrast, have centered on suffering and have been unable to alleviate it. Judaism and Christianity have focussed on sin—and have been able to reduce both sin and suffering. This is partly because they regard suffering not as an unmitigated evil, but as one of the most creative forces in life.

Collectivists in the Church have ignored that self-denial—which is a form of suffering—plays an important part in the divine economy. Instead of accepting free will and sin as the basic issues for man, they have dealt with a suffering that is seemingly unrelated to these things. In so doing, they have bowed to the religious concepts of the East. They are teaching that sin is *separation from God* instead of *a deliberate violation of his will.* This is a novel and erroneous definition. It confuses the effect with the cause. It makes no sense except to members of an anxiety culture, who are person- rather than value-oriented. It ignores that man has the freedom to destroy his relationship with God. It overlooks that a free man in relationship must bear the consequences of his choices.

A Triune Approach to History and Grace

Here we bring our study to a close. I shall finish with some observations about the part man plays in the divine economy of God. This will include the symbols that are necessary for that activity. It will complete what has been said about history and grace, and about the key elements of freedom and responsibility.

When man has a personal understanding of God, there are only three views he can take of history and grace. One maintains that everything that happens is divinely foreordained. This is the predestinarian view: all that occurs is the will of God. A second view holds that God moves providentially in ordering the course of human events—largely in response to prayer. Such a view requires that at times God is obliged to overrule Himself. The third view holds that both of these seemingly opposed concepts are in some measure true. It believes that history is the record of man's acting—or failing to act—in cooperation with God to achieve His purposes.

Neither of the first two views is adequate, either as a view of God or of man. The predestinarian view makes the mistake of confusing God's foreknowledge with His will. (Jesus Himself has implied that God's will is not done on earth as it is in heaven.) As to the providential view, it is obvious that a Father who gives in to all His children's petitions is subordinating His will to theirs.

Looking at the psychological aspects of these views of history, we can appreciate that the predestinarian view gives no freedom to man. Man is not "in God's image" as regarding God's will. Therefore he can hardly be required to be fully responsible. By contrast, the providential view does not make man fully accountable for the freedom he has. Neither view sees man as the image of God in these greatest of personal traits.

For the most part, the religions that hold these views lie outside the Judeo-Christian tradition. The Jewish and the Christian view of history is one of cooperating grace. Yet the schisms that divided Christianity placed many of the churches into one or the other of the first two camps. The Calvinists took a predestinarian view. They looked to the transcendent Father. While their predestinarianism was not nearly so great as that of Islam, they still had difficulty with freedom. The Roman Catholic Church, by contrast, took the providential view. Its immanentism required it to take the opposite view of grace from that held by the Calvinists. While its sacramentalism safeguarded it from pantheism, it still underemphasized man's responsibility, and tended overly to shelter and protect its members.

A departure from triunity can be seen in the identity-symbols that the two churches used. The Calvinist thought of the Church as a "salvation army," and himself as a soldier under orders. The Catholic, on the other hand, belonged to the family of God. He had been adopted as an infant. Even though he had not been consulted, he was thankful to be a child of God, for it made him a younger brother to the Only-Begotten and a co-heir to heaven's riches.

We cannot quarrel with either of these symbols or views of grace; but we must take issue with the notion that the acceptance of one requires the rejection of the other. Both sets of symbols are givens, and each is rooted in the identity of one Person of the Godhead.

In order that man can be fully free and responsible, the two symbols have to be held as one in paradox. This can be done by appropriating a third concept that is found both in the Old Testament and—in an appropriate variation—in the New. It is the concept of partnership. The Jewish identity-symbol has always been that of a partner of God—albeit a very junior partner. The merits of such a symbol are obvious. Partnership permits more freedom than is allowed a soldier. It requires more responsibility than is given a child. Such a symbolism does not suggest that the Jew can be heir to the Partner's estate. Nevertheless, his symbolism gives the Jew a more compelling motive than the Christian to share in the Partner's work. The Christian is all too easily tempted to say, "My Father will do it"—which is providential. Or his attitude may be, "My Captain has already taken care of it"— which is predestinarian. The Jew is more likely than the Christian to say to himself, "If I don't work along with my Partner I can't expect Him to do so either."

In his sectarian divisions of thought, and in his inadequate use of the symbols he is given, the Christian is still the gentile. He is still, like Esau, undervaluing his own identity and that of his seed. Yet there is another symbol that is a given—and it is one that is given only to Christians. It is found only in the New Testament, and it has all the power that is found in the symbol of the partner. It is the symbol of the steward.

It seems to have been Jesus' intention to convert the Old Testament figure of partnership into a New Testament figure of stewardship. The two figures are not the same, to be sure. The partner was an equal, whereas the steward had more the status of a servant or slave. Yet, in terms of freedom and responsibility, the steward was more than a soldier or a child. He was free, within broad limits, to carry out his master's will. He was also accountable in the broadest possible way.

There is an important reason why we can find the Christian's ultimate identity on earth in the symbol of the steward. The partner symbol belonged to an earlier concept of the divine economy. It was one that looked for rewards only on earth, inasmuch as Judaism has only a vague notion of a personal resurrection. The Christian view was a very different one. The one who aspired to leadership had to be content with a life of servitude. Yet for the steward there was a hope of reward. The Christian was called to a ministry of servitude on earth, but he looked forward to a princely crown. In this, he hoped to follow his Master's example. As a faithful steward, the Christian valued his participation in a divine economy of cooperating grace.

In this economy God is the heart, who foreordains the work that the Christian will do but also gives to His steward providential assistance. Knowing this, the steward does all he can to carry out his Master's orders. He knows that God will give the wisdom to know what is right, and the strength to do it. Moreover, God will do what the steward himself is unable to do. The steward knows that God's part in the economy is to do what no one but He *can* do. Finally, he depends upon God, in His infinite goodness, to set straight His steward's well-intentioned mistakes.

Notes on Chapter Nine:

1. George Foote Moore, *Judaism* (Cambridge: Harvard University Press, 1927), Vol. II, p. 110.

2. Erich Fromm, *The Art of Loving* (New York: Harper & Row, 1956), p. 78.

3. Ruth Benedict, *The Chrysanthemum and the Sword* (Boston: Houghton, 1946), pp. 222ff.

4. Klaus Mehnert, *Peking and Moscow* (New York: New American Library, 1964), p. 25.

5. James Joyce, *Finnegans Wake* (New York: Viking Press, 1947), p. 473.

6. David Riesman, *The Lonely Crowd*, from the preface to the 1961 edition (New Haven: Yale University Press, 1961), p. xxv.

INDEX

213